FAITH
—— *is a* ——
WELLSPRING

JOYCE GRAVES

Copyright © 2024 Joyce Graves.
Author's website: https://www.faithfilledtreasureshope.com

All rights reserved. No part of this book may be reproduced, stored, or transmitted by any means—whether auditory, graphic, mechanical, or electronic—without written permission of both publisher and author, except in the case of brief excerpts used in critical articles and reviews. Unauthorized reproduction of any part of this work is illegal and is punishable by law.

ISBN: 979-8-89031-973-9 (sc)
ISBN: 979-8-89031-974-6 (hc)
ISBN: 979-8-89031-975-3 (e)

Because of the dynamic nature of the Internet, any web addresses or links contained in this book may have changed since publication and may no longer be valid. The views expressed in this work are solely those of the author and do not necessarily reflect the views of the publisher, and the publisher hereby disclaims any responsibility for them.

One Galleria Blvd., Suite 1900, Metairie, LA 70001
(504) 702-6708

To my Lord and Savior Jesus Christ, the giver of life in whom I live, move, and have my being. It is to You that I give all the glory and honor that is due unto Your name. All that I am and all that I will ever be is founded in You. As I have yielded myself to You in writing this book, may You give unto Your people an understanding of the teachings within.

CONTENTS

Introduction vii

My Prayer, My Decree x

Chapter 1   The Measure of Faith 1

Chapter 2   Acknowledging Faith 9

Chapter 3   Developing Faith 18

Chapter 4   Decisions in Faith 27

Chapter 5   Anxiety in Faith 36

Chapter 6   Blind Faith 46

Chapter 7   Exercising Faith 56

Chapter 8   Character in Faith 68

Chapter 9   Pursuing Faith 78

Chapter 10 Wisdom of Faith 88

Chapter 11 Wonder of Faith 98

Chapter 12 Faithful in Faith 108

Chapter 13 Burning Faith 117

Chapter 14 Maintaining Faith 127

Benediction 135

About the Author 137

INTRODUCTION

God is so full of love and mercy until it's really unexplainable. It is His desire to dwell in the hearts and minds of His creation. He wants us to trust Him and believe that He is. I would like to take you, the reader, on a faith journey. This book is inspired by simply knowing firsthand how faithful God is. He has shown me inside the depths of His goodness, and His mercy never ceases. He has invaded my life in ways that cannot be described, and if you, the reader, allow Him, He will do the same for you; but it took perseverance, prayer and trust. With those ingredients, you will arrive at a level of faith you wouldn't know you could possess. If we can believe God, then we began to have faith in what He says, after which, we began to trust Him, and that is truly a path I hope we all find. Trusting God is the most important decision any of us could make because in doing so, our lives will never be the same.

In my previous book *My Journey into the Heavens*, I explained how I was taken into this vast library, and I was shown this book. As with that one, it has taken me years to write about it, years of holding it all inside, patiently waiting until He released me to write. It is my desire to share with the reader all that He has given me and purposed in this teaching. In this book, you will find there are so many aspects to faith, so many stages that we have to develop before we can understand the fullness of what it means to have it. *Faith* is a word we use so freely, but do we understand it? Do we fully know what it means to say we have faith? Do we know all the wonderful things that flow from a life that's governed by faith? Within the pages of *Faith Is a Wellspring*, I will share with you all the things the Holy Spirit pulled the veil back and taught me about faith.

Merriam-Webster defines *wellspring*: a source of continual supply.

The definition within itself, if you allow it to permeate inside your spirit, will start to open doors. So with faith being a wellspring, that means faith is the source of our continual supply—never ending, continuously flowing, constantly supplying the ability for us to trust God.

Hebrews 11:1 states,

> Now faith is the substance of things hoped for,
> the evidence of things not seen.

This is our hope when we are in need of our Father; we can be assured He will always provide that which He desires us to have. All our hopes and dreams should rest within Him, and when we don't have the patience to wait on His manifestations, then we pull from the measure of faith that has been granted to us all.

Romans 12:3 declares,

> God has dealt to every man the measure of faith.

God has given us a portion of what we need to build upon, with faith being the substance of what we hope for; it has to be the origin or I could say the origination and essence of what it is we are trusting God for. It has to be the evidence of what we can't see, holding us in its grasp until we see the fullness of what we are trusting and believing God for.

> So then faith cometh by hearing, and hearing by the word of God. (Romans 10:17)

It is by His very word that we gain strength and power when we believe what we have heard. In doing so, we began to trust Him, and that is when the measure of faith He has given us awakens.

Within these pages, we will delve into some of the mysteries and wisdom that is hidden inside of faith. We will explore the realm of power that comes with belief—when we are able to trust God and believe there is nothing we can't accomplish, and there is nothing that will be impossible for us to achieve. It is my heart's desire that you take this faith journey with me. Be encouraged in knowing, and be empowered with the wisdom of understanding the power of faith. As we walk together through these pages, let us embark on all the wonderful aspects of what He has freely given with the precious measure of faith.

> Jesus answered and said unto her, "Whosoever drinketh of this water shall thirst again: but whosoever drinketh of the water that I shall give him shall never thirst; but the water that I shall give him shall be in him a well of water springing up into everlasting life." (John 4:13–14 KJV)

MY PRAYER, MY DECREE

Abba, bless the reader as only You can. May the hearts of Your people who seek let them find. May You open doors inside of their spirits that no man can close. Let them dwell in the secret place of understanding where knowledge abounds so that they may see what is written within the pages of this book. Allow clarity in their mindsets, giving them wisdom that can only be found in You; and to every reader, may You walk away with a renewed strength and a clear understanding of what it means to have faith. It is in the precious name of Jesus I ask of thee. Amen.

1

THE MEASURE OF FAITH

What is faith? And what is a measure? Webster defines *measure* as (1) an adequate or due portion, (2) the dimensions, capacity or amount of something. God has dealt to everyone the measure of faith according to Romans 12:3. Everyone has been given an adequate or, I could say, due portion of faith. The Bible also says in Hebrew 11:1 KJV,

> Now Faith is the substance of things hoped for,
> the evidence of things not seen.

In other words, faith has to stand in the place of that which we cannot see. It has to occupy the space of what we're seeking God for being the tangible evidence of trust. If we are trusting God and believing Him for anything, then we must have faith enough to know that it will manifest in our lives. There comes a time that we must decide which direction we must take, and we have to determine if that direction will lead us into our destiny with our Lord.

We have to learn to trust God with *all* things, knowing in our hearts His ability to bring it to pass no matter what it is. Faith is that evidence it is simply believing God, trusting Him, and then waiting until the manifestation comes. Having a relationship with our Father gives us a chance to know Him in the fullness of who He is. Then as we began to perceive Him as the gracious God He is, we began to believe, and that is the most important part of all—"believing." You cannot have trust in anything that you don't believe in nor can you have faith in unbelief. We must take God at His word and believe that He is. We will never reach levels in faith without accepting the things God has revealed in His word.

Hebrews 11:6 KJV says,

> But without faith it is impossible to please him: for he that cometh to God must first believe that he is, and that he is a rewarder of them the diligently seek him.

Merriam-Webster defines *impossible* as (a) incapable of being or of occurring, (b) felt to be incapable of being done, attained or fulfilled. I think many of us have missed the gravity of what is actually being said here by glancing over the word *impossible*. Now if I paraphrase here, would it make what is being said more understood? Would some grasp the emphasis or be enlightened on the importance of faith? "But without faith it is impossible to please Him." Please allow me to paraphrase: "Without faith, pleasing God is incapable of being done, attained, or fulfilled." We *cannot* please God without faith—that is a fact. That's how important it is that we have faith along with its powerful companion known as trust.

Do we live our lives in error, thinking we can have God however way we choose to have Him? No, we cannot; He has revealed Himself to us in His Word. He has given us instructions on how to live our lives here in this sinful world, but it is up to each individual to love Him enough to live the life He requires of us. When we can accept and believe in our hearts what He says in His Word, then truly that is the beginning of wisdom. Belief leads us to faith, and faith leads to trust. As we believe God, then we begin to develop faith in what He says, and that's when we begin to trust Him. Trusting God is the game changer for us all.

There is nothing more rewarding and powerful as when we trust in our Lord. Proverbs 3:5 KJV tells us:

> Trust in the Lord with all thine heart; and lean
> not unto thine own understanding.

This is saying we will not always understand God's methods or His way of doing things. It's not going to make sense to us at times because His ways are not our ways nor His thoughts our thoughts as stated in Isaiah 55:8 KJV:

> For my thoughts are not your thoughts, neither
> are your ways my ways saith the Lord.

We will never fully understand the depths in which our Father will take us unless we are willing to go, and even then, the way He chooses to do it may never be perceived in our finite mindsets.

God is a God that's dimensional; He is in every direction at the same time. There is no beginning nor shall there ever be an end to Him. As He watches over us and comes to our rescue on many occasions, He has already worked on our behalf before we can even ask of Him, and it's all done simultaneously at once. We may not see the finished work or the fullness of all He has done until the power of it manifests. Oftentimes we're still asking Him for things He has already done, which truly shows a lack of faith and trust. God has given each and every one a measure of faith of an "adequate portion," but it is totally up to us what we do beyond that. Simply put, the ability to have faith in what we choose is already inside of us. He has given us a portion—in other words a foundation to build on. How much we allow our faith to grow can only be decided by each of us. The foundation has been laid. The questions would be "how will you respond to it?" or "how will you nurture that which has already been given?" Most importantly, "How do we finish what God has started in each and every one of us?"

How I would answer those questions would be we can allow our faith to grow. We delve inside the word of God, and we *believe* all that He says. We allow Him to have the measure back to manifest it unto that which He desires. By no means am I saying hand over the measure back to Him as if we don't want it or need it. What I am saying is we surrender to Him, giving Him free reign in our lives, giving Him permission to nurture us and bring us into the knowledge of what it means to have faith, trusting Him with our desires, making sure they line up with His and what He has decreed. The measure, the portion, the slice of the pie can turn into the whole pie. In essence, our faith can evolve into the fullness of what He wants for us. We can become whole in our spiritual lives—nothing lacking, nothing broken—but we must surrender our hearts, our will, and our mindsets unto a living God that knows all and sees all.

So I say to you, the reader, we take the measure, the due portion of faith He has granted, and we run with it. We must run as fast as we can, leaving the enemy behind in our tracks. Run, knowing there are no limits to our Father. Run, knowing He has given us the ability to accomplish all things of heaven and earth in Him. Run, seeking refuge in Him at every turn, believing He will sustain us in all that we do; and we will become that force, the source of power He seeks for us all. We will be able to walk boldly down the paths He has ordained for us with no fear, only power, which is birthed by faith and trust in an almighty God.

We will have the ability to believe walking blindly through each day not having to see but just believing, operating on trust, waiting for the manifestation of what we're trusting Him for, tapping into the power and dominion that has been granted us, living our lives, knowing we have authority over any situation that would cross our paths, resting in who we are as His children, having the assurance of knowing we can move mountains if the need arises.

> And Jesus said unto them, "Because of your unbelief: for verily I say unto you, If ye have faith as a grain of mustard seed, ye shall say unto this

mountain, remove hence to yonder place; and it shall remove; and nothing shall be impossible unto you." (Matthew 17:20 KJV)

How many of us know how small a mustard seed is? I'll answer—it's very small, and when you look at one, you'll begin to realize the magnitude of what He is saying. Because He's telling us if we had faith as a grain of this seed, not the whole seed but a grain of it, then we could say to the mountains "move"; but I'll ask, "What is your mountain? What needs to move out of your path? What is it that you have the ability to change with the power of just believing and trusting Him to accomplish?" I'll answer that as well—"It's called faith." You have it because He gave each of us a measure. Now what will you do with the measure of faith that has been granted to you?

In James 2:18 KJV, it says,

> Yea, a man may say, Thou hast faith and I have works: shew me thy faith without works, and I will shew thee my faith *by* my works.

I added emphasis to clarify because all this is simply saying is you say you have faith, but I don't see it nor your works, but you will be able to *see* my faith *by* my works. Faith is "action"—simply put, acting on what you are believing; and if we can believe, then God will perform the rest. It is not on us to make anything happen—that's on God. All we have to do is trust that He will, and that's faith in action. We must never think that we have to perform anything that's on our Father; all we have to do is believe *He* can. The only part we play in all this is acting on our beliefs. Bringing it to past is on God.

Once we began to believe and develop trust in God, it strengthens our faith life, and that's all our Father is looking for. As we trust Him, then we realize the ability with God lies with our availability. We must always surrender and freely give unto Him all of ourselves, and in turn, He gives us all of Himself. So let us thrive to become mature in our faith walk with our Lord. We must build upon the foundation that has already been laid for us when He gave us the measure of faith. We can become equipped to take on anything the enemy would try and send our way. Remember, the ultimate decision lies with God whether He allows him to bring anything our way; and if He allows it, we must believe it will always be for our good, and it will always lead us straight to Him.

Chapter 1
Discussion Questions and Overview

Main Question: What "mountain" are you facing right now in your life? Grab a piece of paper, and write down the top three mountains you're facing.

Now this is the most important question you'll ever encounter: *Would you take the action and trust God to move it for you?*

If yes, I'd like to invite you to a relationship with Jesus Christ. Use this prayer as a guide.

Dear Jesus,

I come before You today with these mountains in my heart, desperate for Your help.

I recognize that I cannot navigate the journey of life on my own. This is the reason why *I surrender my will to You*, fully aware that Your way is the way of truth, love, and salvation. I trust that Your plan is perfect even when I do not understand it. I invite You into my heart, Lord, to dwell within me and guide my steps. I surrender all my fears, doubts, and anxieties to you. I place my dreams, my hopes, and my future in Your hands, knowing that You are the source of all goodness and wisdom. I'm glad to have You, and today I declare my faith in You, Jesus Christ, and I choose to follow You as my Lord and Savior.

In Your precious name I pray, amen.

A week from now, we'd love to hear your personal experience where your faith played a significant role in overcoming challenges or obstacles. Go back to this chapter and write three takeaways from this experience and we'd love to hear from you as well. Share it with us at faithfilledtreasures.hope@gmail.com.

2

ACKNOWLEDGING FAITH

In the previous chapter, I talked about God giving each of us a measure of faith.

I wanted to convey the importance of faith in our everyday living. As we go about our lives from day to day, we live with much hope—hope that our plans for us and our families can be accomplished, hopes that our dreams may be fulfilled. We do not live our lives thinking that the goals we set for our future will not be met. We live with a spirit of expectancy from God when we trust Him. We expect for Him to provide us with all He has declared in His word that He would do. We do not live our lives with defeated mindsets when we belong to Him. We live with thanksgiving in our hearts, knowing that our Father loves us with an unconditional love that we may never understand. The very essence of who He is permeates in the lives of His children. We live in anticipation of what He will do from day to day, showing us and demonstrating just what we mean to Him.

We must stand on the promises He has made available to us. He came that we might have life and have it more abundantly (John 10:10 KJV). It has always been His intent to be our God and we His children; never will He ever *not* be God. We have a role in all this, and that is to love Him, have faith in Him, and believe. With that being said, we have to acknowledge our faith. Faith has to be "acknowledged"—a clear testament and acknowledgment of that which we believe.

Merriam-Webster defines *acknowledge*: (1) to recognize the rights, authority, or status of, (2) disclose knowledge of or agreement with. Do we really recognize the rights and authority that has been granted to us with the measure of faith He has given us? Or the power in coming into agreement with the power that works within us?

> Now unto him that is able to do exceeding abundantly above all that we ask or think, according to the power that worketh in us. (Ephesians 3:20 KJV)

This is one of my favorite scriptures because if we really delve into what this scripture is saying, we would see how powerful it is. Then we would realize what has been awarded to us by Christ Jesus. God is able to do above and beyond anything that we could ask of Him or even think for that matter. This is a huge undertaking because we never look at the fact that He is able to do more than we can perceive in our minds, more than we could actually bring together in a thought, and we must never forget the latter part of this scripture—it is according to the power that works within us.

The Holy Spirit unfolded this to me. He said, "Joyce, it is according to how much of My power you will allow to work within you." I have never forgotten that, and I will always believe what He told me. I am a living witness that this is true. We must trust when He speaks, He will never withhold anything from us that He desires us to have. He is a gracious Father, and He will always grant us what He has purposed for our lives.

Matthew 7:11 KJV declares,

> If ye then being evil, know how to give good gifts unto your children, how much more shall your Father which is in heaven give good things to them that ask him?

He has never forsaken me, and He will never forsake you. Even when things were transpiring in my life that I didn't understand, it was all working in my favor.

> And we know that all things work together for good to them that love God, to them who are the called according to his purpose. (Romans 8:28 KJV)

If we love God, then we are called, summoned, granted an invitation for all things to work in our favor whether we understand or not. We must trust Him to know that it will. We must trust the process even if it doesn't go the way we think it should. God knows all things, and He knows what we are in need of when we don't; so if there is something going on in your life right now that you don't understand, I implore you to trust Him and just wait—wait for Him to reveal all that He has purposed. Wait on the manifestation, for it will surely come.

Whatever situation we may find ourselves in, here is wisdom. "The circumstances have to first die that they may live," so when you're feeling hopeless, be of good cheer. If your circumstance seems dead, count it all Joy, for truly He has visited it, and it had to die so that He may give it life. When your faith gets under pressure, James 1:2–4 KJV says,

> My brethren, count it all joy when ye fall into divers temptations; knowing this that the trying of your faith worketh patience. But let patience have her perfect work, that ye may be perfect and entire, wanting nothing.

I love this same scripture in the MSG Bible if you need more clarity:

> Consider it a sheer gift, friends, when tests and challenges come at you from all sides. You know that under pressure, your faith-life is forced into the open and shows it's true colors. So don't try to get out of anything prematurely. Let it do its work so you become mature and well-developed, not deficient in any way. (James 1:2–4 MSG)

Hallelujah! He will unleash inside each of us what we allow Him to. When we accept Christ as our Lord and Savior, He lives on the inside of us.

> But if the Spirit of him that raised up Jesus from the dead dwell in you, he that raised up Christ from the dead shall also quicken your mortal bodies by his Spirit that dwelleth in you. (Romans 8:11 KJV)

Therefore, we belong to Him, and in Him we have a Comforter, a Teacher, a Revealer—one who will bring all things to our remembrance according to John 14:26 KJV. Yes, He lives on the inside of us, but we must yield to Him. He will never override free will. He loves to teach us the ways of our Father, leading us into all truths. We must understand the privilege faith has awarded us if we embrace it and allow it to flourish. Imagine our lives on an invisible wheel turning and constantly moving, always moving from one level to the next in our Lord. So as with faith, we move from each glorious stage of growth in God forward, acknowledging as we go from glory to glory.

We find as we grow in our faith life it gets easier and easier to trust God when He shows us His Majestic ways, when He allows us to see the manifestation of His goodness and mercy. Then we are thrown into a realm with the power of knowing—knowing Him to be almighty, knowing Him to be all-powerful, all-wise, omnipotent, magnificent, and holy. When we get to a place of trust and being able to acknowledge Him for these attributes, then we are truly in a place of peace. We are able to understand the need to have faith so that we may live a life pleasing Him as well as praising Him. Faith shows maturity in our spiritual life, for when our spirits are in tune with the living God, truly it will show up in our daily living. A heart that is at peace with God can find peace with others—a wholeness beyond measure lacking nothing, withholding nothing, giving unto our Father all we have, reflecting His image back to Him, worshiping Him in the beauty of holiness, giving Him the glory that is due unto His name (Psalm 29:2 KJV)

In our daily living, acknowledgement of what we believe and what motivates us concerning our Father should always be front and center. We should be able to stand firm, having the faith to be steadfast and unmovable, never wavering when it comes to what God has promised, knowing it shall be. We do this by accepting with our whole heart who He is and what He says, knowing with every fiber of our being that He loves us and He will always take care of us, fully understanding the privilege and the power that is awarded to us through what Christ did on Calvary, acknowledging wholeheartedly that we will take the measure of faith that was given to each of us and build on that solid foundation, trusting and believing that this foundation will carry us through all life's choices, learning to hold fast to whatever He has said, knowing that what He has purposed for us all shall come to pass. We must walk in obedience, striving to live our lives in accordance to His principles and statues.

He is a magnificent God who delights in caring for His children. He delights in teaching us His ways and providing for us so that we will trust Him. In doing this, we are expounding on the measure. We are pushing it to new heights and new levels. We are making the choice to allow what He has placed in us to flow freely. Once we make this decision, then our faith walk becomes a lifestyle. We begin to live our lives, trusting in God's ability and not our own. We start to see things in a different perspective, not always focusing on the trials we face but focusing more on *Him* as the solution to any of them.

God is very merciful, and it is always in the best interest of His children will we find Him. We may not always understand, and sometimes it seems hard. "I am choosing my words well"— it *seems* hard, but in actuality it's not because the greater our fear, the less we will have faith. We must stand firm in what we believe and hold fast to His never-changing hand. It will always hold us and always be stretched toward us.

Let us strive to acknowledge Him in all His ways, and the Scripture says He will direct our paths.

> In all thy ways acknowledge him, and he shall direct thy paths. (Proverbs 3:6 KJV)

In doing this, we can't go wrong. We are on the path that leads us straight into a life filled with faith and trust, a life that is filled with His glory and favor as it flows through us daily, walking in the abundance of knowing Him to be our Father, allowing the light of His presence to shine bright within us, knowing in our hearts that we can trust Him in all things, striving to learn of Him as we go about our lives, daily seeking to do that which is pleasing in His sight, living our lives, knowing that we can do all things through him, knowing there is nothing that shall be impossible to us if we can only believe. We must allow this to be birthed in our hearts as well as our mindsets. That is why He tells us to be transformed by the renewal of our minds.

> And be not conformed to this world: but be ye transformed by the renewing of your mind, that ye may prove what is that good, and acceptable, and perfect, will of God. (Romans 12:2 KJV)

We must allow Him to turn our mindsets toward Him and help us perceive the things of Him and not of this world. This helps us prove His will is good and perfect when we follow after Him and not the world. We must walk boldly in the knowledge of who He is and who He is to us. I can stand firm with assurance and declare He is my Lord and Savior and His Spirit lives within me. As His children, we should all be able to declare this with authority and power. We must base all our choices on what we can believe Him for, taking everything to Him in prayer, knowing that He cares about every aspect of our lives, consulting Him *before* making life-altering decisions instead of trying to find Him in the midst of something we never included Him in. We should seek Him first and trust Him to lead and guide us through all life's choices. As we do this, it is truly a testament of "acknowledging our faith."

Chapter 2
Discussion Questions and Overview

This chapter teaches us how we need to acknowledge our faith. It teaches that our lives should be a testament of our faith walk. We should live with a spirit of expectancy when it comes to God, allowing Him to show forth His abilities within us, making all our decisions based off His will and purpose for us, consulting Him before making choices that has life-altering consequences.

1. How has acknowledging your faith and trusting in God's promises brought peace and maturity to your spiritual life?
2. Can you share a personal experience when trusting the process and having faith in God's plan made a difference in your life?
3. How can you transform your mindset to focus more on God's ways and less on the ways of the world?
4. Are you willing to trust in Him and His ability and allow Him to teach you what is means to have faith in Him?

3

DEVELOPING FAITH

It is our desire to grow and mature in our Lord. We want to increase in knowledge, always striving to understand spiritual matters. We should never just want to scratch the surface when it comes to God. We should all want to go deeper into the water when it comes to Him because that is where He calls unto us. Deep calls unto deep according to Psalm 42:7 KJV. It is His desire that we have an intimate relationship with Him, knowing His commands, and keeping His ways, surrendering our will unto His good and perfect will, knowing what our Father requires of us gives us the ability to obey Him and live our lives walking in obedience.

There is nothing more powerful than His children being in direct obedience to God. Nothing can withstand the power and authority this grants us. The Holy Spirit revealed this truth to me one day when He said, "The power lies within obedience." God desires us to obey Him because in our obedience, we walk in His righteousness. Christ learned obedience, and so should we.

> Though he were a Son, yet learned he obedience by the things he suffered. (Hebrews 5:8 KJV)

Living our lives in direct obedience to God will help us in developing our faith. One of the many definitions for *develop* is to evolve, synonyms and similar words being to *unfold*, *grow*, *progress*, *emerge*, and *mature*. All these words have one common denominator—they all signify growth. Faith has to evolve within us and come to a level of maturity that takes us beyond the boundaries of unbelief. We must first ask ourselves this one question: "Is anything too hard for God?" This is often misquoted from Jeremiah 32 when it's said,

> Jeremiah asked, "Is there anything too hard for God?"

The question was not asked by Jeremiah; the question was asked by God. Jeremiah stated what he knew to be a fact—he perceived Him as the sovereign Lord as he declared this in verse 17:

> Ah Lord God! Behold, thou hast made the heaven and the earth by thy great power and stretched out arm, and there is nothing too hard for thee. (Jeremiah 32:17 KJV)

When you get to verse 27, God is the one who asked the question when He stated,

> Behold, I am the Lord, the God of all flesh: is there anything too hard for me? (Jeremiah 32:27 KJV)

I can answer that with a surety—*no*, there is nothing too hard for God, and we should be able to declare it like Jeremiah. We should allow our faith to be developed to the point of being able to know in our hearts that this is the truth. It is only when we can perceive Him in this manner that we will reach the level of maturity we would need for our faith level to rise. In order to know God, we must learn of Him, as I stated earlier: Make it intimate. Make it personal. Seek His ways, and in doing this, it will all start to become clearer. He will not withhold Himself from us nor will He turn away from a heart that seeks Him.

> And ye shall seek me, and find me, when ye shall search for me with all your heart. (Jeremiah 29:13 KJV)

He wants each of us to find Him and learn of Him. There is a clear path that leads to him, given straight from His Word.

Whatever we would desire to know about God, the Bible teaches us—all His commands, all His attributes, all His standards, and most importantly, His principles. God is God, and He does not change. He is the same God today, yesterday, and forevermore, but do not be deceived in not knowing His methods change. He will not always come the same way in His teaching, but His love is everlasting, and His truth will never waver. Sometimes He will hide inside our purpose, desiring for us to seek Him.

As He taught me, "I will hide in the spot of your purpose so that you may seek Me and find Me there, then you shall be where I have purposed for you to be." I have never forgotten that, and I shall always teach whatever He reveals unto me. Everything He reveals to us can always be found in His Word.

> It is the glory of God to conceal a thing, but the honour of kings to search out a matter. (Proverbs 25:2 KJV)

Will you search for Him? Sometimes we may feel we can't find Him or that at times He is silent. When this happens, search for *Him*. He knows where we are, but do we know where He is within our lives? Are we where He desires us to be in Him? That is a personal question that we must all answer for ourselves. Oftentimes we miss what God has for us because we are not where we need to be and we won't follow His instructions to get there. He will not withhold anything from us. Why won't we ask of Him? He will grant our request, but sometimes He has terms that come with some things and conditions as well. Sometimes we have to act—or should I say *ask*—to get results.

> Ask and it shall be given you, seek and ye shall find, knock and it shall be opened unto you. (Matthew 7:7 KJV)

> If ye abide in me, and my words abide in you, ye shall ask what ye will, and it shall be done unto you. (John 15:7 KJV)

This one should grab us all:

> If any of you lack wisdom, let him ask of God, that giveth to all men liberally and upbraideth not: and it shall be given him. (James 1:5 KJV)

For more clarity, from MSG Bible, the same verse:

> If you don't know what you're doing, pray to the Father. He loves to help. You'll get his help, and won't be condescended to when you ask for it. Ask boldly, believingly, without a second thought. (James 1:5 MSG)

The latter part of this verse in James 4:2 KJV states, "Yet ye have not because ye ask not." Do we really know what it means to *ask* of God? I know how to ask of God, and if you, the reader, will allow me to teach you how to ask, it will change your life. Asking God is not just going to Him asking for a request and you can't even believe He will grant it. You will never receive of Him in that manner. Remember Hebrews 11:6 KJV when it says he that comes to God must first believe that He is.

Before we ask anything of Him, we must first believe He is able to perform it, and we must believe we are able to obtain it. To ASK in an acronym is A (assurance) and S (simply) K (knowing). When we come to our Father to ask anything of

Him, we must have assurance of simply knowing that He will accomplish that which we ask. When we make a request, we must believe that what we are asking Him is already done *before* we can even ask. Remember Ephesians 3:20 KJV:

> Now unto him that is able to do exceeding abundantly above all that we ask or think.

So that means He is able to perform above anything before I can ask or even think it. When we can come to God with assurance in our hearts, knowing when we ask of Him it has already been granted, then we have found the doorway to asking.

Believing before we can even see the manifestation grants us into the realm of the power in asking. If we can trust God and believe, then we are able to make our request known to Him through prayer and supplication.

> Be careful for nothing; but in everything by prayer and supplication with thanksgiving let your requests be made known unto God. (Philippians 4:6 KJV)

Most of us, when we read this scripture, don't focus on the word *thanksgiving*. In *Merriam-Webster*, it's defined as "the act of giving thanks or expressing gratitude," so I'll paraphrase here:

> But in everything by prayer and supplication giving thanks and expressing our gratitude we make our request known unto Him.

Would it be safe to say we are already thanking Him and expressing gratitude to Him before we even ask when we do this? Couldn't I take that to believe that if I'm thanking Him before I ask, then I already believe it to be granted ? If we do what we are instructed to do in this scripture, He is teaching us how to ask of Him. Trust and believe it to be done, being thankful before we ask, then it shall be granted. As we mature in Him, our faith begins to grow—or I will say again it begins to develop.

Developing in our faith is simply surrendering unto Him, allowing Him to show us the fullness of who He is and who He can be in our lives. As we grow in the knowledge of Him, we begin to mature. We become more aware of His plans and purpose for our lives. We begin to obtain wisdom in spiritual things as He teaches us how to take on all the tricks and snares of the enemy. We begin to recognize his schemes and techniques. God will allow us to be mindful and watchful, knowing that the battle does not belong to us. Victory is already ours. We do not have to fight in a battle that was over before it began. It is through Christ Jesus that we obtain everything. We do not have to fight for dominion—it was granted back to us by what transpired on Calvary—and through Christ, we will always wield the power and authority He has given.

Victory is knowing we have the power, the means, and the ability to fight, but the wisdom of God allows us to know we don't have to because through Christ we already won. Christ bought back power and dominion for us on Calvary when He gave His life as a loving sacrifice freely given. He did not have to die for us, but He did. He did not have to pay the price that sin demanded, which was death, but I'm so grateful He did. He made it possible for us to have all that is rightfully ours. Everything that was stolen in the garden of Eden was granted back to us through Calvary. Now lies within us the ability to love Him in return, the ability to trust Him and believe; and most importantly, a measure of faith was granted so that we could take this measure and allow it to develop. This can be something so wonderful and something so powerful if we allow it to birth in us.

If we allow our faith to develop, we can become the powerful beings God created us to be; after all, we were made in His image, after His likeness. We are fearfully and wonderfully made as stated in Psalm 139:14 KJV. He gave us something that in turn helps us fulfill what He wants from us. He gave us a measure of faith, and faith is what we will need to move any obstacles out of our way. He tells us if we have faith, nothing is impossible unto us (Matthew 17:20 KJV).

So what are we waiting for to allow our faith to flourish? What are we allowing in our lives that would hinder us from developing in our faith? Those are questions that each of us can only answer for ourselves, and what's so wonderful, we can start today as I will go over in the next chapter. We can make the decision to allow our faith to develop. We can decide to start right here, right now, today developing in our faith.

Chapter 3
Discussion Questions and Overview

This chapter teaches how to develop in faith, how our faith needs to flourish and grow. Victory in our Lord already belongs to us. We have a clear path that leads straight to Him. All we have to do is yield ourselves to Him and obey.

Developing in our faith is simply approaching God with assurance that He will perform all that He has said, asking Him for whatever we desire, and then trusting and believing that He will grant it to us.

1. What does it mean to develop faith, and why is it important in your personal relationship with God? *Share your thoughts on how faith evolves and matures over time, and discuss the significance of deepening your faith beyond surface-level beliefs.*
2. How can we apply the concept of "asking" with assurance and thanksgiving in our prayers to develop our faith? *Reflect on the acronym ASK (assurance, simply knowing), and discuss how believing that your requests are already granted before you ask can impact your prayer life.*
3. What steps can you take to seek a deeper, more intimate relationship with God in your daily life? *Explore the idea of seeking God within the context of your unique purpose, and discuss practical strategies for drawing closer to Him and recognizing His presence in your life.*

4

DECISIONS IN FAITH

The life we live is about choices. We choose which direction we will take every day. We don't always make the right choices because oftentimes, we don't consult God when we make them. Accepting Jesus as our Lord and Savior will be the most important decision we could ever make in this life. Living the life He requires of us takes patience with others and even ourselves. We don't always get it right every time, but He is always there to lead us, guide us, and teach us all truths. He came that we may have life and have it more abundantly, says the latter part of John 10:10 KJV:

> The thief cometh not, but for to steal, and to kill, and to destroy. I am come that they might have life and that they might have it more abundantly.

But I ask of you, the reader, what do you perceive to be an abundant life? Is it fame, fortune, or materialistic endeavors?

Do you view abundance as personal gain, or is it something shared among others? God wants us to live our lives being amply supplied with all we need. I hate to rain on anyone's religious parade, but an abundant life has nothing to do with money, fame, or anything materialistic. God desires us to be abounding and plenteous in spiritual things. All the things that come from Him is what needs to be overflowing in our lives. He desires us to live free from the bondage, tricks, and snares of the enemy. That is why He told us in John 10:10 KJV what he came to do for us. He told us what the enemy desires to do to us, and then He tells us what He desires for us. Our Father knows if we abound in our spiritual life, it's hard for the enemy to overtake us. Because when we know who we are in Him, when we know the power that's within our reach, we are that force to be reckoned with.

We can live with assurances, knowing that He will supply all our needs in accordance to His riches as declared in Philippians 4:19 KJV:

> But my God shall supply all your need according to his riches in glory by Christ Jesus.

He is able to perform all that we could trust Him for through Christ. As His children, there will never be a time that He would withhold anything from us. He desires us to grow into maturity in Him, learn of Him, seek Him, and most of all freely come unto Him and receive all that He has. We must be as pitchers before a full fountain, ready to be filled, ready to overflow with the knowledge and revelations that can only come from Him.

God is merciful and mighty in *all* His majesty, in *all* that He does, and He desires for us to have *all* of Him *all* that we can embrace, *all* that we can perceive it's ours—a love so freely given unto us it cannot be measured on our standards—and the riches I speak of "according to His riches" are priceless, a peace that surpasses all of our understanding, joy that is unspeakable, with divine authority and power, wisdom and understanding, discerning of spirits and knowledge beyond all that we know on earth. Those are things that can't be bought nor can they be obtained outside of our Lord.

In all this, it goes back to the choices we make. We have to decide that we will give our lives to Him. We have to decide that we will allow Him to govern our lives and so with our faith.

We have to make decisions in faith. Oftentimes, I will define words because I desire the reader to have an understanding of what I'm trying to convey. Sometimes you have to know what words mean before there can be clarity. *Merriam-Webster* defines *decision* as (1) the act or process of deciding, (2) a determination arrived after consideration. So a decision is what we determine after careful consideration on any thought process, then whatever conclusion we come up with, we base the final outcome on that which we have decided to do on the matter. As with our faith, we have to decide whether we will trust God. We have to weigh all the evidence and make a decision based off what we *can't* see, therefore rendering ourselves slaves not unto fear but power.

FAITH IS A WELLSPRING

Once we can give ourselves over to God enough to take Him at His word, just believe we tap into the realm of trust. Each of us has to make a decision in this faith walk because it cannot be determined by anyone else. I cannot decide for you nor can you decide for me how much we as individuals will trust God. Within the realm of faith, there are so many possibilities, so many doors that we must walk into to fully understand what faith is, and making decisions in faith causes us to realize we no longer belong to ourselves but we belong to Him. There will be times in our lives we don't understand what God is doing nor where He is taking us, but we must make a decision to trust Him and go. We don't always get to decide or even determine the outcome of trials we face, but we can decide to trust Him with it.

Where we are in our faith walk is where we choose to be. God has granted us the ability to take what He has given and then allows us to choose how much we allow Him to elevate us and govern our lives. In faith, there will always be a deciding factor because we can choose to trust God or we can choose to try it on our own. His ways will not always be how we think it ought to be because oftentimes, we have predetermined what we think God should do and how He should do it. No, my brothers and my sisters, this should not be so. We have got to come to a place where we know in our hearts that He knows what's best for all of us. Why wouldn't we trust the one that holds tomorrow in His grasp to lead us there Himself? God knows what each of us need before we can even think it. He has it all prepared before we realize there even is a need. Why won't we give Him the honor that is due unto Him? Why can't we accept the power that is granted to us by being His children?

If we give something to our children, knowing it will help them, knowing it will give them power to overcome, how would we feel if they did not use it? We possibly grieve the Holy Spirit when there are so many resources we have from Him and we don't use them. It is His desire to lead us, to teach us, to comfort us, to give us wisdom and knowledge, to bring all things to our remembrance.

> But the Comforter which is the Holy Ghost, whom the Father will send in my name, he shall teach you all things and bring all things to your remembrance, whatsoever I have said unto you. (John 14:26 KJV)

According to John 14:16 KJV, He will abide with us forever. He will always be there for us because our Father sent Him to us—the Spirit of truth. We have all we need to live abundantly; we have all we need to trust our Father and allow our faith to grow beyond the measure that was granted.

God is relentless. He will not stop until He achieves what He wants from us all. He will not give up on any of us as sometimes we give up on ourselves. We often build walls in our lives and then get discouraged when we can't climb them. Then we get even more discouraged when friends and family can't climb them either. We were not born to climb walls or mountains that seem to get in our paths, nor are we to try and find ways around them. We are His children, and in that aspect, it grants us the right to power and authority. Therefore, we can use that power that we wield with our mouths and speak to them, causing them to crumble at our feet, and the God we serve will allow us to walk through the rubble on solid ground. Hallelujah.

So in essence, let us believe. Let us decide to take our faith to new levels in Him.

Let us make the decisions in our faith that will always lead us right back to Him, learning to trust in His ability and not our own, learning to trust when it doesn't make sense to trust, learning to believe when there's no reason to believe and all we have to rely on is His Word.

There is nothing in plain sight. There is nothing except our mindsets and what we can trust our Father for. There will always be a place of divine purpose, and we all must find it, but I can promise you it will not be found in unbelief. The probability of pleasing God will never be found in a heart that does not believe. The very essence of who we are is founded in Him. The ability to believe is already inside of us—we actually have to make a decision not to believe. We have to decide not to have faith in anything, and in making that decision, we will come full circle to the end of ourselves; and once we come to the end of ourselves, we fully realize that's where He begins; and when we allow Him to begin, that's when we decrease so that He may increase in us.

The more we allow Him to lead and we follow, the more powerful we become because we are walking in direct obedience unto Him. God is so merciful, and He is omnipotent in all His ways—brand-new mercies we see every single day. All we have to do is place our trust in Him and allow Him to pull us higher and higher in our faith. As we grow, our faith level grows, and there is never an end to what God can and will do for us. He desires to teach us on this journey so that we will abound in His love and grace, but we cannot experience the glory of who He is without faith. We cannot reach the depths He desires for us without trusting Him enough to believe in all that He does.

So I beseech you, the reader, to do all you can and make the decision to allow your faith to develop. Allow it to become the weapon you will need to walk through this life. We are tossed and driven by things seen and unseen, and it gets hard to focus sometimes. We must learn to hand Him the things we don't understand, give Him our worries, lay them at His feet. If we tell our situations how *big* our God is, then we will realize just how *small* they are; and in doing so, we began to focus more on Him than the troubles we face. So let us decide to trust, decide to believe, making the most of what our Father has given us, determining to walk in the fullness of who we were called to be as His own, standing boldly, proclaiming the word of truth, and the God of all creation will never leave us.

He will always grant us the ability to make our own decisions, desiring us to choose His way and His will for our lives, pointing us in the right direction, but we have to yield and obey. We have to surrender our will unto Him, going forth with a spirit of expectancy, waiting to see the manifestations of our trust in Him. God will always love us with an unconditional love that we will never be able to understand here, but when we are finally with Him, all we have endured will not matter because we will know fully who we are and who He is.

> For I reckon that the sufferings of this present time are not worthy to be compared with the glory which shall be revealed in us. (Romans 8:18)

I like the way it reads in the Amplified Bible:

> For I consider [from the standpoint of faith] that the sufferings of the present life are not worthy to be compared with the glory that is about to be revealed to us and in us! (Romans 8:18 AMP)

Oftentimes I'll use translations from other Bibles other than KJV, and this is only for clarity for readers that have trouble following the King James Version of the Bible. God has so many ways to give unto us what we need, and it is His desire that we all be able to find our way to Him. I always try to teach with a clear understanding so that what God is trying to convey through me is received *and* perceived. My ministry is what God has given me, and I am commissioned to give unto His people that which He has given me. All that He reveals to me I shall teach it, and if one person can see Him in the light of who He is by my teaching, then it will not have been in vain because I trust Him to do in me what He has purposed for me, and that is how we must approach Him, having faith enough to believe all will be accomplished within us. In doing this, we learn to make good sound decisions in our faith.

Chapter 4
Discussion Questions and Overview

This chapter teaches how we are to rely on our Father for all things. It teaches how we are to make decisions concerning our faith. We can live the abundant life He offers us, but it is not earthly abundance. The power and authority that lies within us cannot be purchased because it was already bought on Calvary. God desires us to have all that He has declared we can, but it requires us to live our lives in accordance to His plans and purposes. We have the ability to choose whether we allow Him to pull our faith level higher. In essence, we have to make the decision to go.

1. Think about a significant decision you've had to make in your faith journey. What led you to make that decision, and what was the outcome?
2. How did trust and belief play a role in that decision, and did it lead to a deeper connection with God?
3. If you made the decision to trust God and believe list some ways that He showed you how faithful He is.
4. Tell us as a testament of your new found decisions in faith, what would you say could best describe your motivation?

5

ANXIETY IN FAITH

In our lives daily, we face challenges. We often hear people quote "trials come to make us strong," but where is that strength when we face something that seems to shake the very foundation of where we stand? Where is the strength that so many speak of when we feel our backs are against a wall? I'll tell you where that strength is, and it is found in Christ Jesus.

> I can do all things through Christ which strengthens me. (Philippians 4:13 KJV)

We were never meant to face any of life's challenges alone. He promised never to leave us nor forsake us (Hebrews 13:5 KJV), but what do we do when we *feel* like we're falling or failing, when it seems like all is lost? Or like the lyrics in the song "Even If" by Mercy Me when it says, "What will I say when I'm held to the flame like I am right now?" But the lyrics don't stop there—it continues with this declaration: "I know

You're able and I know You can save through the fire with Your mighty hand, but even if you don't, my hope is You alone."

I love this song because it is a testament that we should trust God no matter what it looks like or how we feel, and even if we're in the fire, we must still trust in His ability to bring us out; and we can rest assured if He allows us to be in the flames, there is something that needs to be burned off us. Hallelujah! When we're feeling like no matter where we turn we're being crushed on our jobs and even in our everyday living, that is when we trust. That is when we grab hold to the hem of His garment and not let go. We can only find refuge in Him. No matter what we may face, no matter what comes our way, God always has the answers, and it is only when we can take our eyes and focus off the situation do we find the ability to trust Him.

As long as we focus on it, then it becomes bigger and bigger, for we are feeding it with fear and anxiety, which does not come from God.

> For God hath not given us the spirit of fear; but of power, and of love, and of a sound mind. (2 Timothy 1:17 KJV)

As long as we are fearful of anything, it becomes larger than it actually is. He did not give us a spirit of fear, but He never said we would not experience it. It is what we do with fear when it arises that determines the outcome when it comes to faith. Sometimes we all face things that makes it hard for us to trust God at first, but as we grow in Him as our faith evolves, we begin to realize where we get our power and our strength. We must never get to a point in our lives where the fear of anything outweighs our faith. Jesus asked in Mark 4:40 KJV,

> And he said unto them, "Why are ye so fearful?
> How is it that ye have no faith?"

There will be times we experience anxiety in our faith, with *anxiety* being defined as "apprehensive uneasiness or nervousness," "strong desire sometimes mixed with doubt, fear, or uneasiness."

We will sometimes find it hard to trust God. We get caught up in the illusions of how things seem to be—what it looks like, what it feels like, or even what is said about it. God is the ultimate Judge of everything; He has the final say, the authority in all things seen and unseen. We need to find a way to trust Him in all aspects of our lives—be it with our families, friends, even with our jobs. He knows what we need before we do.

I know it's hard sometimes on our jobs because we might feel He's not concerned in that area, but He is. He wants to be the one we turn to and seek refuge. He wants to be the one we trust with everything. When we trust Him, we can rest assured that He will perform all that we can trust Him for. There are times when circumstances outweigh our belief, but we must quickly dispel those doubts and fears when they surface. We must quickly rid our minds from that which is not in our hearts.

Faith drowns fear as a wave when it overtakes the shoreline. Faith must cover fear, snuffing it out, leaving it no room to breathe, therefore rendering fear powerless to us. It seems at times we allow the level of the problem to determine the outcome for us. *Stop* right now, and make a decision not to walk this path. No matter how it seems, God is always with us, and He is always in control of everything. He is working on our behalf when we don't even realize it. I make the statement all the time: "God will not work for us." Strange thing to say but true—*He will not* because if He works for us, then we think we have the ability to dictate the outcome. Isn't that what bosses do? We think we have the right to tell Him what to do, help Him out, so to speak, but what He will do, He will work on our behalf in our favor, but we must first believe that He can and He will. He will allow us to make the decisions whether we can perceive it.

Know this from a person that has walked this path—faith is born inside of us—and what I mean by that is the measure that He gave us all has to be birthed inside us. We have to labor to get to the point of fulfillment. My faith developed from the things I have had to endure. I have not always been in this place of trust—I actually had to fight and war with myself to get here—because believe it or not, it is the fleshy part of us that desires to make war with our spirits. Our spirits will always trust God because we were born of God.

> Beloved let us love one another: for love is of God; and every one that loveth is born of God and knoweth God. (1 John 4:7 KJV)

If we live from our spirits, we will develop that same trust and belief. We won't have a problem taking God at His word and just believing. Our spirits will always be in tune with God because that is the part that came from Him.

> And the Lord God formed man from the dust of the ground, and breathed into his nostrils the breath of life. (Genesis 2:7 KJV)

All that we are, all that we have comes from Him, but we are given the ability to choose our way. Trusting God, I can honestly say it is a place of rest, assurance, and wholeness. I can stand in the fullness of who I am and declare He has been my rock. Even when I don't understand, I trust Him. When it doesn't make sense, I trust Him. When it seems like all is failing and it can't possibly work in my favor, that's when I dig in and trust Him more. That's where the power lies within our ability to stand firm in the fire and know that He has us safely in His arms. When we can be still in any given situation and know that He is God, then we prevail. I have faced so many trials that I felt I couldn't make it through, things that I thought would level me. In the midst of all of them, He was right there, but it was only afterward that I could see His hand.

We must find a place inside our spirits that we connect with our Father. There must be a spot that is reserved for Him alone, and then we must learn how to go there and wait for Him. Wait when we need Him and cry out to Him. Wait for Him to draw us unto Himself as we hide under His wings. Psalm 91:1 says,

> He that dwelleth in the secret place of the most High shall abide under the shadow of the Almighty.

Hiding inside His shadow, inside the image reflecting from Him, there is refuge as well as strength, and that is how we take all our anxieties, all our problems, and leave them at His feet, making the decision that in all my worries, in all my fears, Father, I will allow my faith to rise to a level of power. I will allow my faith to supersede anxiety. We know there will be times that we will have doubts and even fears. During those times is when we hunker down and tell the enemy we will not bow down to his illusions, tricks, and snares.

We will not focus on what is presented to our eye gates. We will walk blindly, allowing our Father to order our steps. We will make decisions to plant our feet on solid foundations whether we can see them or not. We have got to have blind faith, which I will discuss in the next chapter—nothing to go on, nothing to be seen or heard, just totally believing and trusting Him to be God. Worrying will not change a situation, but trusting in our Father will. Standing on His promises is the game changer. Applying His Word to our lives truly leads us down the paths of stability. Being anchored in our Lord is a newfound peacefulness that only His own will find. We are the sheep of His pastures. Surely He will provide and protect us in this sinful world. God is a dependable God. There is nothing we can't trust Him for.

The love He has for us is indescribable nor will we ever understand it. It's unconditional; there is no hidden agenda nor anything that props it up. It is as solid as He is. We will never know the depths, nor will we comprehend the reach, because it will find us no matter where we are. We must trust and believe in the power of it, believing that it will conquer anything in our lives. We must choose faith over fear, allowing faith to absorb anxiety. Cover it like a blanket. As I said, snuff it out so that we cannot have doubts about God's ability to perform that which He has said. God is able to accomplish more in our lives if we yield to Him and follow the paths that He set our feet on.

> The steps of a good man are ordered by the Lord
> and he delighteth in his way. (Psalm 37:23KJV)

He directs our paths; therefore, we have nothing to be afraid of. He delights in giving unto us, demonstrating the love He has for each of us, and He will most certainly lead if we will follow. He will guide us through traps and snares that are placed in our paths by the enemy.

We can boldly request as in Psalm 119:133 KJV:

> Order my steps in thy word and let not any iniquity have dominion over me.

He is faithful to perform all we could ask of Him, but we must have enough faith to believe He can, and we must trust and believe He will. God is calling us all to a place of refuge. When He gave us the foundation of where faith lies within us, we have the power to build off that foundation. We have the power to move anything from our path if we can believe Him for it and not doubt. We find ourselves willing to trust God with simple things, which seem not so hard to accomplish in our perception, but where is the faith in that? What happens when everything is literally crumbling around us and it feels like there's no way through it? When everything we can see goes in the opposite direction of what God is saying to us?

I can answer that with a surety—we must allow our faith to move up to another level. Make the decision to trust God no matter what it looks like. Let faith be our tangible evidence of what we can't see. Allow faith to stand in the gap, and believe God for what we think is impossible. Truly this will change our lives because we will tap into a realm of faith we never knew existed, and once we're there, we won't allow anything to pull us from that spot. Because it is a place we can hear Him clearly, we can receive instructions without question. We don't always have to know why God does what He does; all we have to do is obey. It's not going to make sense to us all the time, and when it doesn't, go with Him—He's God. He doesn't owe us an explanation for anything, but He loves us enough until sometimes He will give us one. Let us love our Father in return, showing Him how much we appreciate all that He has done and all He does daily on our behalf, operating from a place of pure trust and belief, knowing with Him, all that we can believe shall be manifested to us if we don't doubt.

I leave with you, the reader, the power and knowledge to know inside of you there are rivers that flow. These rivers are ready to take you on a journey as they flow freely through your spirit. The Living Water lives within us, ready to wash our spirits and replenish us, guiding us back to who we really are.

> He that believeth on me, as the scripture hath said, out of his belly shall flow rivers of living water. (John 7:38 KJV)

As He told the woman of Samaria,

> Jesus answered and said unto her, "Whosoever drinketh of this water shall thirst again: but whosoever drinketh of the water that I shall give him shall never thirst; but the water that I shall give him shall be in him a well of water springing up into everlasting life." (John 4:13–14 KJV)

Therefore, we have nothing to fear; all we need to do is believe. Again I'll say believe that He can, and I beseech you to believe that He will; but my questions would be, "Will you allow your faith to close the door on anxiety? Or will you allow fear and anxiety to outweigh your faith? Which as children of the Most High God fear and anxiety—those attributes truly has no place in our lives unless *we* allow them access.

Chapter 5
Discussion Questions and Overview

This chapter teaches to not allow anxiety and fear to keep you from trusting God and believing what *He* says. He never promised fear would not arise, but He did declare He didn't give it to us. It teaches what to do when we find ourselves in the midst of situations and circumstances that cause anxiety. We make a decision to trust and believe. Fear does not determine faith. Always apply this principle to all of life's challenges and choices. We must always allow faith to overpower and snuff out fear.

1. What are the three major situations in your life that were filled with anxiety and fear?
2. How did you handle the experience, and did your faith play a role in alleviating your anxiety?
3. What lessons did you learn from that experience, and how did it impact your trust in God?
4. Within your own experiences, were you able to hold on and allow faith to shield you?
5. Have you been able to apply what you have learned so far about faith in your life? If so, how?

6

BLIND FAITH

In our lives daily, we have to fight not to walk in the realm of sight. We have to war with our flesh on a day-to-day basis not to operate on that which we can see. We often find it hard to trust God because what we're able to see in a situation outweighs our belief; therefore, we find it hard to have faith in it. If we find ourselves in this spot, we must move and move quickly. We cannot trust God, believing only on what we can see with our natural eyes. We must come to a place that we trust Him no matter what it looks like, and that's where faith abides. When I speak of the realm of sight, I mean anything that can be seen with our eyes in this realm. If we choose to live from this perspective, the enemy will always defeat us because he is the master of illusions. There will always be something he will entice us with based upon how it looks to us or how it feels, and oftentimes, if it is pleasing to our sight, we delve into it without thought or consideration of the consequences. We become slaves to our desires and wants based upon the same conception how they make us feel or what they look like. We need to approach faith from a spiritual aspect and not from a carnal one. If we perceive faith as something God gave us, a gift even, then we would understand how precious it is. We would begin to understand the importance of maintaining our faith, which will be discussed in a later chapter. We must have blind faith, unable to see it, unable to understand it, unable to explain it but most of all unable to trace the origin. We will never be able to perceive where faith starts in us nor shall we be able to say it will have an ending.

Because just when we think we have all the aspects of faith, there is always more. Hence, the title to this book, *Faith Is a Wellspring*. Faith is a source of continual supply, constantly supplying us with what we need to live a life that is pleasing in God's sight, constantly pulling us deeper into the water and moving us to doors that can only be opened inside of faith. We must come to learn the power that faith wields. What can be impossible for us if we can believe and take God at His Word? The latter part of Matthew 17:20 KJV states that nothing shall be impossible to us if we have faith. With faith, we have the power to believe, and we have the power to trust. We can choose to walk on a straight and narrow path before our Father and live by faith.

> For therein is the righteousness of God revealed from faith to faith as it is written, The just shall live by faith. (Romans 1:17 KJV)

Yes, we can choose to live by faith and reap all the benefits that comes with it. Even when Jesus healed in the Bible, He told them it was according to their faith. Whatever the circumstance, it is always what we can believe God for, or can we allow ourselves to trust Him to accomplish it?

> Then touched he their eyes, saying According to your faith be it unto you. (Matthew 9:29 KJV)

That lets me know it's according to what we can believe and have faith in. If our faith can stand as evidence until we receive the manifestation, then we can have what we trust Him for. There are so many scriptures where Jesus demonstrated the importance of faith. In individuals or even with mothers, fathers, friends, He always told them how great their faith was and it was their faith that caused them to receive.

How many of us has glossed over Mark 11:22 KJV:

> And Jesus answered saying unto them, "Have faith in God."

I have to be honest that scripture had not stuck out to me until the Spirit of God is teaching me about faith. Jesus said, "Have faith in God." Could we not say this is a command? Or could it be viewed as a direct instruction? Either way, it is something that if we obey, it will lead us into a realm of power and authority. Having faith in God and trusting in His ability and not our own makes all the difference in all our circumstances. We have to come to a place that we just believe, and all we have to go on is because He said it. I remember an instance when I was taken in the Spirit realm and He showed me how we must walk a path that is so straight but narrow, blindly trusting Him. I was in this beautiful mansion, and I started walking through a room that seemed to have no end to it.

The more I walked, the more narrow it became. As I was walking, I noticed the walls were closing in on me from both sides, but I kept walking. Soon all I could do was walk straight because the walls were touching my shoulders on both sides. After the walls began to touch my shoulders, I came to the end of the room, and I had to step up about five steps into a hallway lined with doors. I was standing in front of the first door on the right, and I heard the voice of the Lord telling me to open it and come in the room. I immediately obeyed and opened the door. I was not prepared for what I saw because upon opening the door, the room did not have a floor visible. I could see walls and a ceiling, but there was no floor, just a black hole where the floor should have been.

I heard the voice of the Lord again. He said, "Come into the room."

I hesitated and said, "Lord, this room has no floor."

He said it again: "Come into the room."

I said, "Lord, this room does not have a floor."

He said, "Are you sure?"

I said, "Lord, I do not see a floor."

He said, "Just because you do not see a floor, does that mean there isn't one?"

I said, "No, Lord."

He said, "Then come into the room."

Without any more hesitation, I made the decision that I was going to trust Him and His ability because surely if He told me to come into a room that I couldn't see a floor in it, He had the power to sustain me. I stepped into the room, and to my amazement, I was standing on a solid foundation. Although I still could not see a floor, I was standing on one. I looked around, and I was standing in front of a desk. Then I heard the voice of the Lord say, "Now the student is truly facing the Teacher, and when the student faces the Teacher, then can the student be taught."

I have never been able to forget that. He showed me if we walk the straight and narrow path, it will lead us to blind faith. We will be able to trust Him and what He says even when we can't see our way. Even when it doesn't make sense, we will still follow the voice of our God, trusting and believing whatsoever He says. There was no floor visible, but I had a decision to make. I could have refused to go in, choosing to act solely on what I couldn't see, or I could do as I did—trust God in His ability to take care of me. If He tells us to do anything, we can be assured that provisions have already been made. When He led me to the room, everything was already accomplished for me before I got there; all I had to do was believe Him. He taught me firsthand that we can't rely on how it looks or how it seems. We must obey His voice no matter what. All I had to go on was His voice and His instructions. He told me to come in the room, and I told Him there was no floor because I could not see one.

Even though I still couldn't see a floor, I obeyed Him, but it was after he posed the question which left me with a decision to make. I could decide to trust in my own ability, thinking there was no floor because I couldn't see one, or I could trust Him and believe that there was a way I could come in the room. I made the decision to step into blind faith with nothing visible to help me believe. I decided to trust in what He told me and acted upon it, and that is how I approach any situation that I have no control over. I choose to trust *Him*. I will acknowledge to Him this is bigger than me, this one belongs to you, and all I have to do in this is trust you. We have to know when to let God be God. We have to know when there comes a time that we must be still and know that He is God.

> Be still, and know that I am God: I will be exalted among the heathen, I will be exalted in the earth. (Psalm 46:10)

We have to understand that it's never by our own strength that things are accomplished in our lives. It is by His strength that abides in us that makes us able to stand firm and walk boldly in who we are by way of Christ. All we have to do is tap into the realm of faith, blind faith, trusting faith, and nothing shall be impossible unto us. We must move beyond what others think we can do. Never allow anyone to determine your ability to trust God and have faith in what He says. Never ever base your faith on what someone else believes. I cannot determine your faith level nor can you determine mine; we must all believe God for ourselves, and if I choose to walk blindly, allowing Him to order my steps, then it will be a choice that I would make, and each individual has to choose their path—the one God laid out for us or the one we choose for ourselves and walk in it.

Keep in mind there will be no forcing in the matter. "Free will" is the determining factor in all our lives. A God of nothing but love will never force any of us under submission. We must come to Him freely, loving Him as He loves us, freely choosing to embark on what faith holds for us. How could what I'm about to say ever make sense unless you can perceive it from your spirit? Faith is tangible; it can be seen.

> When Jesus *saw* their faith, he said unto the sick of the palsy, "Son, thy sins be forgiven thee." (Mark 2:5 KJV, emphasis added)

Faith must be the evidence of what we're hoping for and the evidence of things *not* seen, but it must be blind. Yes, we must have "blind faith," nothing to go on to make us believe but trusting and believing because He is, having faith in Him because He's God with no other reason to accept anything other than because He *said* it.

Let us build our hopes and dreams on the Word of God, walking blindfolded, so to speak, allowing Him to order our steps. Blind faith is never having to see before we believe, when we have nothing to base our trust on other than the fact that He is God, never wavering although we can't see anything, never doubting even when it seems all hope is gone. Blind faith is trusting and standing in His ability and not our own while we wait. Wait with a spirit of expectancy, knowing in your heart that He is able to do above anything we could ask or even think. Wait, having the assurance of knowing it doesn't matter what it looks like—the manifestation will come. We will always prevail with faith.

In every circumstance, we will grow higher and higher, getting valuable wisdom. Because in all our experiences concerning faith, we will always find another level after the one we have fulfilled, always increasing.

> And the Apostles said unto the Lord, Increase our faith. (Luke 17:5 KJV)

And that is the most rewarding part because we will never arrive to the end of faith. Just as there is no end to God, there is no end to faith.

> I tell you that he will avenge them speedily, Nevertheless when the Son of man cometh shall he find faith on the earth? (Luke 18:18 KJV)

There will always be someone willing to trust God as there will always be someone allowing Him to move their faith beyond the measure. The ultimate decision lies with each of us, but how will we ever know what God will do for us if we don't trust Him? If we don't give Him a chance to show us who He is, how will we ever know Him?

What will it take to spiral us over into faith if we don't put faith in action? At some point, to reach the level of faith that God would desire us to have, we have got to put our trust in Him and just move forward with a spirit of expectancy. Move forward, seeking His will for our lives and even when we can't see His hand. When we don't know what direction to take or how to go forward, we must ask of Him. Ask for His guidance. Ask Him to reveal the path unto us and give us clarity and then wait—wait on the manifestation of what you're asking of Him. This will teach us how to trust Him, and it will also give us the assurance we need to help us trust Him more. As we do this, it becomes easier and easier to seek Him for guidance, for strength, and most of all an understanding. As I have said, we will not always know where God is taking us on this journey, but we have to be willing to go, nor will we always understand; but as we develop trust out of our faith, then we begin to realize just how faithful He is.

Can we submit ourselves to Him enough to walk in blind faith? Can we surrender enough to tread in deeper waters, desiring to go past the boundaries of unbelief? Because that is where the power and authority lies. That is where we will find there are no limits; there is no place in Him we cannot go if we allow Him to usher us there. When we yield to the pull on our spirits to come unto Him and experience His amazing love and grace, when we walk in the fullness of who we can be in Him, we begin to demonstrate that power. We begin to trust Him for things that men would say are impossible. We see solutions instead of problems. We see the end and not be overwhelmed by the beginning. We see what we're trusting Him for and not what we're observing. When we get to this stage, it is here that we find we're able to walk in the realm of blind faith.

Chapter 6
Discussion Questions and Overview

This chapter teaches the importance of trusting God and believing Him no matter what we may see. We must live our lives based off what the Word of God says and placing all our trust on His truths, walking in the fullness of our faith, believing for things we deem impossible. Within blind faith, there are no limitations placed on our beliefs. We believe despite what we may see. We trust no matter where we find ourselves. We walk in the realm of knowing, not having to see in order to believe.

1. Can you recall a specific situation in your life when you had to exercise "blind faith," where there seemed to be no visible solution or way out?
2. How did you approach that situation, and what were the results of your trust in God's guidance and His unseen plan?
3. The chapter emphasizes the importance of walking in faith even when you can't see the way forward. What steps can one take to nurture and strengthen their "blind faith"?
4. Can you share any personal experiences or strategies that have helped you cultivate this level of trust and belief in God?

7

EXERCISING FAITH

What comes to mind when we say exercise? When we hear the word, we immediately think about physical activity of some sort. Exercise has several meanings, but in the capacity I'm speaking, *Merriam-Webster* defines it as "the act or an instance carrying out the terms of an agreement (such as an option)." So in essence, to exercise our faith means we will carry out the terms of the agreement God stipulated concerning faith. Faith is an option for us; we have to make a decision whether we embrace it. We have to actually choose to carry out the terms that comes with the measure of faith He gave to us. We were given a portion of something so wonderful, which is beneficial to each one of us.

> Now faith is the substance of things hoped for, the evidence of things not seen. (Hebrews 11:1 KJV)

He is telling us what faith is. So with these terms, do we agree and act upon them, believing that this is what faith is?

Or do we choose not to come into agreement, choose not to believe and have no faith? Let's look at this same verse in the MSG Bible:

> The fundamental fact of existence is that this trust in God, this faith, is the firm foundation under everything that makes life worth living. It's our handle on what we can't see. (Hebrew 11:1 MSG)

Hallelujah! This is exactly what faith is—tangible evidence of things unseen. We can hold on to our faith in God, allowing it to be what we need until He brings the manifestation.

As God's children, we have a right to believe Him for the impossible. We should allow no one to determine this. We must put our faith to work, allow it to stand up against any unbelief. When we have trouble trusting God or believing Him for anything, this cancels out faith in the individual, not all. I can't have faith for you, and you will not be able to determine faith in me.

> For what if some did not believe? shall their unbelief make the faith of God without effect? (Romans 3:3 KJV)

I can answer that *no*, by no means shall we ever be able to determine the power in what God does. Just because a person cannot perceive the things of God or when we don't understand, it does not change the outcome of what God intended. The faith we can have in our Lord will always be effective, but each individual has to make that choice for themselves.

If we find ourselves in a place where we don't understand, then we need to ask of Him.

> If any of you lack wisdom, let him ask of God, that giveth to all men liberally and upbraideth not; and it shall be given. (James 1:5 KJV)

Same verse MSG Bible:

> If you don't know what you're doing, pray to the Father. He loves to help. You'll get his help, and won't be condescended to when you ask for it. Ask boldly, believingly, without a second thought. (James 1:5 MSG)

He loves when we ask of Him. He loves to give unto us. We need to seek His face for all things. Putting our trust in Him changes the whole outcome of any situation. When we lack in our understanding, He will teach us and lead us into wisdom and knowledge. Utilizing this weapon of faith He has given gives us the power and ability to look at life's challenges and face them head on, allowing us to not be intimidated by the tricks and snares of the enemy because we are already defeated if he can get us to focus on any situation and not on Christ.

We have got to come to a place where we can actually see Christ in the midst of the storm, making a conscious decision to trust Him no matter what it looks like. When we can view any circumstance in our life exercising our faith from the beginning, we will always have the victory. Oftentimes we have had to go through things we wouldn't ordinarily have if we had trusted God *first*. If we would have enough faith to believe that He is able to fix whatever the problem is, then we would be utilizing and acting upon the measure that was given—but that can only be decided by us. We can choose to exercise our faith, or we can accept the situation at hand. We can put our faith into action and believe that we have the power to change any circumstance. We have the ability on the inside of us to trust God for anything and know that we can do all things through Him.

> I can do all things through Christ which strengthens me. (Philippians 4:13 KJV)

When we make the decision to walk in the power and authority that faith has awarded us, then we can see the manifestation of this power. I know this to be true because in Luke 8:22–25 KJV, we read the story of Jesus getting into the ship with His disciples, and as they sailed, He fell asleep. In the midst of Him falling asleep, the Bible says there came a storm of wind on the lake, and they were filled with water and were in jeopardy.

Then they went and woke Him up, saying, "Master, Master we perish."

Jesus arose and rebuked the wind and the water. Everything ceased, and it was calm, but the first thing He asked them was, "Where is your faith?" But they wondered among themselves, asking each other, "What manner of man is this? For He commands the wind and water, and they obey Him."

Jesus was demonstrating that if they had faith, they could have done the same things He did. It is possible—I am a living witness to this truth. I have spoken to the wind. I have spoken to storms and have watched them calm down and cease. I remember my husband and I were on a cruise, and we were coming back from the Bahamas. For some reason, the sea was turbulent, and the waves were very high, hitting against the side of the boat. We had an ocean-view room, and I could see the waves out the window as well as feel the motion of the ship. I got up off the bed and made a decision I trusted and believed what I was about to do because I had done it several times. I had faith enough to believe that it was my right to take such authority as a child of God.

I went up on the lido deck, and if you've never cruised, that's a deck on the top of the ship. I walked to the railing with the glass petition and stood looking out over the sea, and these were my words: "I do not know what has caused this in you. I do not know what has you so turbulent, but I'm going to need you to calm down." I said, "Waves, you are too high, and I command you to calm down. In the mighty name of Jesus, I command you to cease and desist." I stood there with a spirit of expectancy because I know who I am and I am aware of the power that's in our mouths. I am aware that it is our birthright as His children to do as He told us we would do. He said greater works we would do if we can believe.

> Believe me that I am in the Father, and the Father
> in me: or else believe me for the very works' sake.
> Verily, verily, I say unto you, He that believeth

> on me, the works that I do shall he do also; and greater works than these shall he do; because I go unto my Father. And whatsoever ye shall ask in my name, that will I do, that the Father may be glorified in the Son. If ye shall ask any thing in my name, I will do it. (John 14:11–14 KJV)

Jesus is letting us know if we believe in Him what can be accomplished by the power of faith and belief. So much more clarity from MSG Bible:

> Believe me: I am in my Father and my Father is in me. If you can't believe that, believe what you see—these works. The person who trusts me will not only do what I'm doing but even greater things, because I, on my way to the Father, am giving you the same work to do that I've been doing. You can count on it. From now on, whatever you request along the lines of who I am and what I am doing, I'll do it. That's how the Father will be seen for who he is in the Son. I mean it. Whatever you request in this way, I'll do. (John 14:11–14 MSG)

I stood on that deck, expecting to see the manifestation of my faith in action. I was expecting to see the very atmosphere shift because I know when we speak with authority, believing and trusting God for what we have spoken, it shall be. I stood there and watched the waves begin to get smaller and smaller as they stopped hitting against the side of the boat. I watched them die down to a gentle wave instead of a crashing one. I watched the sea do as I had commanded it, and that was to calm down. The joy I felt was indescribable. Just knowing we belong to God and knowing He has given us authority is priceless. We are His, and we have dominion as well as power and authority here on earth. All power of heaven and earth was given to Jesus on Calvary. When we accept Him as our Lord and Savior, then the authority is granted to us.

One thing I learned that I speak of in my previous book *My Journey into the Heavens*, everything God created is a living and breathing entity—the water, the wind, the atmosphere itself—so if those things are alive and we have dominion over all things, why wouldn't they obey us *if* they recognize the authority when we speak?

Remember, Jesus said, "Be it unto us according to our faith."

> Then touched he their eyes, saying, According to your faith be it unto you. (Matthew 9:29 KJV)

I did not doubt that I could speak to the wind. I did not doubt I could speak to the waves. I believed I could. God has taught me and allowed me to demonstrate the power in my mouth on many occasions. I choose to exercise it. I choose to exercise my faith. I know without a doubt that many would think you're crazy to talk to a sea, but I know without a doubt we can. We can speak to the very elements, and they have to obey.

On another occasion, I was sitting at my desk at work, not really aware that a storm was upon us. One of my coworkers kept looking out of the window behind me, but I didn't think it strange. Finally, she got up and came to my desk and said, " You don't see what it's doing outside?"

I said, "No, what are you talking about?"

As I asked her the question, I stood up and turned around and looked up. The windows behind my desk were up high next to the ceiling. When I looked out the windows, all I could see was black clouds. I turned back to her and asked, "What the world…how long has this been going on?"

These are the words she said to me: "This storm came out of nowhere so fast, and I told myself, 'There is no way Miss Joyce know this is going on and has not moved from her desk.'" She has watched me speak to the elements so many times, and she has seen what God allowed to manifest. She clearly believed if I spoke to it that it would cease because her words were, "Miss Joyce, you need to open your mouth."

I remember walking toward the front door, and as I looked out, I could see it had started to rain. The wind was blowing really hard, and the trees had started to bow you could see small limbs on the ground. I walked outside under the covered walkway in front of the office, and I began to look around. I started talking to the clouds first, then I began to address the wind and then the rain. I commanded the clouds to release what was in them but not in a way to wreak havoc. I commanded the wind to cease from blowing in a manner that would cause destruction. Then I commanded the rain to cease from pouring so hard, causing problems with visibility. I stood there again as before with a spirit of expectancy, having enough faith to know that what I could trust God for, He was able to perform it. The wind began to die down first, then the rain started to ease up. It was moving out as quickly as it came.

When I stepped back into the office, she was looking at me, and she said, "Miss Joyce, I'm scared of you."

I told her, "There is nothing to be afraid of. You can do the same thing if you can just believe that you can."

There is never anything to fear when it comes to God. We should always know as His children, we have the power to command the very elements if we tap into that realm of faith. When Jesus said greater works we would do, He meant it. If He could calm a storm, why can't we do it? Why can't we trust Him enough to believe what He said? Oftentimes we talk ourselves out of what we're able to do because we deem it to be impossible before we even try. We talk ourselves out of the probability of some things before we even get to it. I call that "self-defeat"—we have defeated ourselves before we can even believe we can accomplish something.

We should never remain here if this is where we find ourselves. Never doubt God to the point that we cancel out all He is able to do, before we even allow Him the chance to show us He can. If we never trust Him with anything, then how will He be proven to be trustworthy? Everything about God is sure. Everything that He has decreed shall be. Nothing is impossible for Him if we can believe for it. There is nothing that we can't accomplish through Him—all it takes is faith. If you don't believe you can talk to the wind, then surely nothing will happen because there is no power in unbelief; but if you can take God at His word, stand boldly, and place a demand on anything, trusting and believing, then it shall be granted to you. God is faithful to perform all that He has said—it is up to us to exercise our faith enough to believe it.

So I say to the reader do not limit the God we serve. Do not place limitations on Him. He is more than able to do anything that we can trust Him for. Step out of the familiar, and just believe and not doubt. Remove yourselves from the comfort of accepting things as they are, and start speaking what can and will be. Use the power that God has granted us in our mouths. Life and death is in the power of our tongue.

> Death and life are in the power of the tongue:
> And they that love it shall eat the fruit thereof.
> (Proverbs 18:21 KJV)

We have the ability to cause life or death with the words we speak. We can speak life and cause a situation to live and thrive, or we can speak defeat, which causes a situation to die. Words are powerful—especially the Word of God.

When we speak His Word, believing what He has said, nothing shall be impossible to us. God's word will not return to Him void; it will accomplish all that He has purposed for it.

> So shall my word be that goeth forth out of my mouth: it shall not return unto me void, but it shall accomplish that which I please, and it shall prosper in the thing whereto I sent it. (Isaiah 55:11 KJV)

There is nothing God says He will do that we could ever say He can't or won't do it. I'll always give more clarity because I desire an understanding—same verse, MSG Bible:

> So will the words that come out of my mouth not come back empty-handed. They'll do the work I sent them to do, they'll complete the assignment I gave them. (Isaiah 55:11 MSG)

God is faithful in His Word; it is up to us to exercise our faith and just *believe*.

Chapter 7
Discussion Questions and Overview

In this chapter, we embrace the aspect of putting our faith in action with faith being the substance of things hoped for and the evidence of things we can't see. It teaches we can believe this and, therefore, accept the terms of this agreement. We can make declarations to believe God and all that He has said and promised. We should never doubt God and cancel out all that He would do for us with unbelief. The chapter highlights the concept of exercising faith as a choice to believe and trust God even when circumstances seem impossible.

1. Can you share a personal experience where you had to consciously choose to exercise your faith and carry out the terms of your faith agreement with God?
2. What were the results of your decision?

I encourage readers not to limit God and to speak words of faith, trusting in His promises. How can you incorporate exercising faith in your own life, and what specific steps can you take to grow in your ability to believe in the seemingly impossible based on God's Word?

8

CHARACTER IN FAITH

The essence of who we are can sometimes be defined as our character. This is who we are—our attributes, in other words. Our characters are features that distinguish us as individuals. They define us so much that each of us are sometimes judged by this very attribute. God needs to be seen in all our characteristics—the love of who He is must flow through each of us daily—so if we must maintain our character in our daily living, why can't we realize it goes for faith as well? Faith is the substance of things hoped for; then it's safe to say faith must be *the* substance. Faith must fill a spot, bridge the gap for our unbelief until we can trust God, but what are we allowing to flow from our faith? What are we showing forth concerning faith? Are we exuberating fear or trust?

Fear cannot abide with faith, for one will cancel out the other. We have to decide which one we will allow to manifest. The main character in our faith must be to believe, and out of that belief, trust will come forth. Trust will be produced when we can lean upon the words of our Father. We must learn to accept what He says and obey His commands. Everything God gives to us, we can be of assurance it is what's best for us. We often forget the promises He has made to us, trusting in our own ability. Where trust lies, then the doors are opened unto us that have been locked by fear and anxiety. We must trust in all that He has purposed for us, knowing that we shall have whatever *He* says we can have.

Knowing God and the fullness of who we can be in Him makes all the difference.

We should be known by the fruit we bear.

> Wherefore by their fruits ye shall know them.
> (Matthew 7:20 KJV)

Who we are will show up in our daily living. What's inside of all of us will show up on the outside. When we trust God, He knows it, and that opens up avenues we will never find when we don't. We must seek God with our whole heart. In doing this, we will find there is so much of Him we miss out on, and I have to be quick to say it's not on His end because He's always knocking.

> Behold I stand at the door and knock: If any man hear my voice and open the door I will come in to him, and will sup with him and he with me.
> (Revelation 3:20 KJV)

I love to quote from the MSG Bible for those who need more clarity. Same verse:

> Look at me. I stand at the door. I knock. If you hear me call and open the door, I'll come right in and sit down to supper with you.

God is saying, "I stand at your door and knock. I will come in if you allow me to, and I will do unto you and extend the same as I did with them."

This is symbolic of the last supper He had with His disciples in Matthew 26–28 KJV:

> And as they were eating, Jesus took bread, and blessed it, and brake it, and gave it to the disciples, and said, Take, eat; this is my body. And he took the cup, and gave thanks, and gave it to them, saying, Drink ye all of it; for this is my blood of the new testament, which is shed for many for the remission of sins.

All we have to do is yield to Him our wants and desires, and we can be sure that when we do, everything will line up with *His* will and *His* way. When we can trust Him, then we learn the characteristics of our faith. We find how deep of a level we have. We learn what distinguishes our faith and how we allow it to grow. Faith is ever changing; it's always moving, always evolving to new levels and new heights and depths in Him, with the main characteristic being belief—we must *believe* God in all that He says. He is God, and He knows all things of heaven and earth, so why won't we believe in Him? Why not trust the one who not only knows what tomorrow holds for all of us;

He knows how we will respond to it. I have trusted God with some impossible situations in my life—or so it seemed. At the time, I saw them as such, but I had a decision to make—either I could trust God no matter what it was looking like, or I could succumb to what my eyes were seeing.

I chose to trust Him, and in doing that, I found He was working in my favor all along. When we develop a history with God—and what I mean by that is we look back over what He has done in our lives—we then begin to develop trust. In all the circumstances that followed, I made the decision to trust Him. Based off past encounters, when another one came, I remembered what He had done before. Therefore, I was able to rely on past experiences to help dictate future experiences. He is the same God. If He brings you through one thing, He is more than able to do it again. If we need to go back and remember to tap into our history with God, so be it. If that's what it takes to build your faith, then by all means, do it. All it takes is making the decision to trust Him, and it will grow from there. Remember, the measure is already inside us. The ability to trust is already there; we just have to decide whether we will use it.

God will never call us to something or set a door before us that we cannot enter.

He will never set us up for failure in our lives. As His children, He always wants us to have victory and abundance in all things. There will never be a time that He would cause us to fall. More often than not, He has to pick us up out of ditches we have created for ourselves and others. We must have character in faith showing forth the desire to lay it all at our Father's feet and just believe. Being humble is a characteristic that we must embrace. Patience needs to follow close behind. With both of these attributes, we place ourselves in a position that God can use us for *His* glory. We will find ourselves seeking ways to honor Him and not ourselves. We will yield and be of service unto His people, acting out of kindness that flows from our hearts, loving our neighbors as we love ourselves, which is actually a command.

> Thou shalt love thy neighbor as thyself. There is none other commandment greater than these. (Mark 12:31 KJV)

Obey His commands and live our lives so that we may please Him, bearing the fruit of the Spirit found in Galatians 5:22 KJV:

> But the fruit of the Spirit is love, joy, peace, long suffering, gentleness, goodness, faith.

So how many of us has looked at faith being a fruit of the Spirit? As I stated in a previous chapter, faith is action; it's tangible. Have you ever really taken time to look at the order of these fruits of the Spirit? Love comes first then we have joy, which the joy of the Lord brings peace and strength. Once peace abides in our spirits, we develop long-suffering and then gentleness. Then the goodness of God invades our life, and standing at the end to swallow them all is faith. Faith will allow us to love. It will allow us to have joy in our Lord. We will find peace. Faith in our Father will cause us to be long-suffering just as Christ is, which leads to gentleness and kindheartedness, showing forth a love for our God and others that surpasses all our understanding.

We need to exuberate all these characteristics in our faith, releasing the power of who we are and who He is in us. God is just to perform all that He has decreed for us. All we have to do is make ourselves available to Him, and the work is already done. He places us strategically in the lives of others so that we may perform that which He has set in motion. We cannot walk this walk and not be of service to others. What would that show of our character? The essence of who we are will manifest. It cannot be hidden, for sooner or later, it will surface. We are the ones to determine whether we will allow these characteristics to abide inside our faith, our belief, our trust in the Father. We have the ability to have faith in God and allow the fruit of the Spirit to govern our lives.

We will find they will work better through faith because inside of faith, we will yield more to these attributes. We will trust God enough to allow them to flow freely through our lives, embracing the fullness of what these fruit will produce for us. God is obtainable to each of us, and having faith in Him gives us the ability to dive deeper into the water. I am speaking of the Living Water, our Comforter, our Teacher, the Spirit of the Living God. In Him we can live, move, and have our being (Acts 17:28 KJV). We can learn to receive and accept all He has granted to us. Our desires will line up with His desires for us, and we will walk that straight and narrow path He has laid, striving to fulfill all He has purposed for each of us. God's plan and purpose for us is always perfect, but we don't see it that way at times. That's where faith comes in. We have to learn to trust Him no matter how it seems.

Because what we can perceive could be so far from where God is taking us until we miss the mark, we must put our trust in Him, put our faith in first gear, and wait, move forward with a spirit of expectancy, knowing that He is able to accomplish all that we are trusting and waiting for, allowing the characteristics of our faith to show forth in full bloom, allowing others to see the manifestation of what God can do in all our lives when we wait. We already know He is able to do more than we could even ask or think for that matter, but the miraculous part is how He will show himself strong in us and through us if we allow Him to.

The essence of who we really are lies with our Father, and He will allow each of us to know just where we are in Him. Allowing the characteristics of our faith to show moves us to a place of total surrender unto our Father. We must yield to His power and yield to His plan for us as we mature in our faith. Authority lies with every believer, and the power that having faith in our Father gives to us moves mountains. We must accept it, embrace it, obtain it, and live it, totally understanding that we must walk in obedience to Him, acknowledging Him to be the sovereign Lord that He is, accepting without question all that He has made available to us as His children.

We must allow His Spirit to govern our lives as we move from level to level in our faith because the higher the level, the deeper the growth and more accountability. What I mean by that is the deeper we go in our Lord, much more is required.

He expects us to hold a standard for others to see Him in our lives so that they might find their way.

Luke 12:47–48 KJV says,

> And that servant, which knew his lords will and prepared not himself neither did according to his will shall be beaten with many strips. But he that knew not and did commit things worthy of stripes shall be beaten with few strips. For unto whomever much is given, of him shall be much required.

The more God entrusts us with, the more He requires of us. When we belong to Him, our lives are not our own. Believe it or not, we are here to serve and be of service unto each other. We must do as Christ did when He came to the earth be about our Father's business. We must strengthen each other when we learn how to mature in our faith, teaching others how to allow theirs to grow when they don't understand how to yield to God concerning faith because once we begin to surrender our trust to Him, then we begin to believe Him for things we deem to be impossible. Trusting God, as I have said, gives us the power and ability to stand firm on a solid foundation. It gives us the ability to move forward and not worry because we know He is with us, watching over us in all things, desiring a heart to have faith in all He does and all that He says.

This begets maturity on a whole new level. Think on this—as we grow in life from one stage to the next, so shall we do in faith. We cannot allow our faith walk to become stagnant. If so, we will begin to settle and revert back to what we can see instead of trusting God. We begin to lose the ground we have covered and then become a target for the enemy to come and try and pull us further backward. We must stand firm in what we know and encourage and pray for each other when we feel we're getting to a place where our faith begins to waver.

> But I have prayed for thee, that thy faith fail not: and when thou art converted, strengthen thy brethren. (Luke 22:32 KJV)

When we feel our faith wavering, never be afraid to acknowledge to God; when we're feeling this way, He knows, and He will strengthen us. This in turn still shows our faith in Him, in His ability and not our own. He loves when we come to Him, acknowledging things and telling Him how we feel; after all, He already knows, but this shows a trust in our Father and a desire to be led by Him.

Chapter 8
Discussion Questions and Overview

This chapter places emphasis on the characteristics that are displayed inside of faith. What are we allowing to flow from faith in our lives? Are we allowing fear or any type of negativity to be the catalyst of what we can believe? It allows us to see we can trust God; He will never lead us into failure. It teaches that our faith can lead us into a place of total surrender, yielding more to His attributes, teaching us to stand firm and mature in our faith, therefore allowing us to grow from one level to the next; and as we do this, we gain strength, and it gives us the ability to strengthen others. This chapter also emphasizes the importance of faith as a characteristic of our character, one that distinguishes us as individuals.

1. How do you think the characteristics of your faith are reflected in your daily life and interactions with others?
2. What steps can you take to ensure that your faith is characterized by trust in God and a desire to live out His will and display the fruit of the Spirit in your life?

We can gain strength by trusting in God, having faith, and showing forth this characteristic:

1. Share with us ways after you've been strengthened in your faith that you could help to strengthen others.
2. Sometimes circumstances may cause us to get discouraged. In those times, what are some steps you could take if you feel your faith beginning to waver?

9

PURSUING FAITH

We live our lives every day in pursuit of something, be it promotions on our jobs, wholeness in our families, or just plain acceptance from others. We're always trying to obtain more, which in essence we have all we will ever need. It has always been mankind's quest to know and explore things seen and sometimes those things that are unseen, hence seeking psychics and mediums. Granted the invisible realm is far more real than this one, but we do not need those types of people to tell us our future—God already has—and if we can trust the word of a psychic over the word of God, we have far greater issues that need to be dealt with quickly. We do not need to try and sneak in the back door when He's standing at the front door knocking. All we will ever need is founded in Christ Jesus. Everything He has purposed and promised we have access to it.

But why do we constantly want more, seeming never to be satisfied? Why do we search for things that are empty and vain, things that do not benefit us one way or the other? The one that cripples us the most is we are always in pursuit of happiness, which is shallow within itself. God gives us joy, as we saw in the previous chapter, and is a fruit of the Spirit, so it's safe to say the Spirit of God produces joy as one of the attributes that flow from the Spirit.

Another area of pursuit that causes despair is when we seek acceptance from others, which we will quickly find pleasing others should never be at the top of the list. Living our lives in a way that would be pleasing to God should be first and foremost. If we find ourselves in pursuit of so many other things that does not matter, I ask the question, Why can't we be in pursuit of faith?

What does it mean for us to be in pursuit of our faith? Does that mean we have to search for it? What are you really asking, Joyce, if you're saying we need to be pursuing faith? To answer, *no*, we do not have to search for faith because we all have already been given a measure of it. One of the definitions for *pursue* is "to find or employ measures to obtain or accomplish, to proceed along." So when I say we need to be pursuing faith, all I'm saying is we need to look for ways to mature our faith. We need to move forward to obtain and accomplish all that God desires for us to find inside of faith. When I say look for ways, get inside His Word, and see what He says about faith. Learn the benefits of having faith in God. Begin to understand the power that lies with us when we get to a place of trusting God and just believing.

Don't be satisfied with the measure because there are so many depths and levels in faith. Don't stop seeking to understand what faith grants us. Keep moving forward; a measure does not stop. An inch becomes a foot, a foot becomes a yard, yards become feet, and so on. So as the measure God gave us with faith, it has no limits, no restrictions. We can have all God has given, but it's up to us where we stop. We will never encounter a stop sign from God in pursuit of Him. He desires us to seek Him, to search for Him, but most importantly, it is His desire we *find* Him—and find Him we will because He will not withhold anything from us. As I've said—and I know I sound like a broken record—He is obtainable; we can have all of Him. He wants an intimate one-on-one with us, drawing us unto Himself, revealing the power of knowing Him for who He is.

Once we have faith in Him, we begin to *know* Him. We begin to understand the importance of yielding our mindsets and our hearts to Him. The more we trust Him, the more tangible spiritual things become to us, and we find it easier and easier to accept what He says without question as to *why* and *how*. He knows what we need. He knows what it would mean for us to have the type of faith He desires for us all. The power we wield by trusting Him cannot be measured; it is the catalyst that leads to so many dimensions in Him. Faith moves mountains, and there are a lot of mountains that we will face in this life. How much more easier for all of us if we are able to do what He says we're able to do if we had faith the size of a grain of mustard seed.

> And Jesus said unto them, "Because of your unbelief: for verily I say unto you, If ye have faith as a grain of mustard seed, ye shall say unto this mountain, Remove hence to yonder place; and

it shall remove; and nothing shall be impossible unto you." (Matthew 17:20 KJV)

We could speak to these mountains, and they would have no choice but to move. How is that for power and benefits in having faith? Another way we can pursue faith is to first ask ourselves do we understand what faith is? We cannot be in pursuit of anything if we don't even know what it means. If we don't understand the magnitude of the power in faith, how could we allow it to evolve in us? How would we ever understand what God needs or wants from us concerning our faith if we do not pursue it? How could we allow it to magnify and become the powerful tool God meant and purposed for it to be if we don't embrace it? In order to go after anything, we must first know what we're looking for. If we don't seek God and realize the power we wield with faith, we'll never fully understand what faith is. If we don't yield our life to Him by way of trust, how will we ever find the door that unlocks the measure?

To unlock the measure, we must first have an understanding as to what faith actually awards us. I know to be in pursuit of something, we must try to fully understand it. God wants us to understand all the aspects of faith and what it grants us. He desires that the veil be pulled from our eyes concerning faith that way we'll know what He is calling us into.

> That the God of our Lord Jesus Christ, the Father of glory, may give unto you the spirit of wisdom and revelation in the knowledge of him: the eyes

of your understanding being enlightened; that ye may know what is the hope of his calling, and what the riches of the glory of his inheritance in the saints. (Ephesians 1:17–18 KJV)

These verses in the MSG Bible clarifies it for better understanding. It reads:

I ask the God of our Master, Jesus Christ, the God of glory—to make you intelligent and discerning in knowing him personally, your eyes focused and clear, so that you can see exactly what it is he is calling you to do, grasp the immensity of this glorious way of life he has for his followers. (Ephesians 1:17–18 MSG)

When the eyes of our understanding are enlightened, which simply means when we can perceive or comprehend something, then we will begin to realize God is actually in pursuit of us. He is relentless as I have stated. He will not give up on any of us, and He won't stop until he has us because He loves us so much. His love for us knows no bounds, and He will reach into the depths of darkness and pull us out—a love that supersedes all we could ever imagine, something so freely given to us all.

Faith leads us to the very heart of God because it teaches us to trust Him. We won't always be able to see what God is doing on our behalf, and I believe He sometimes hides it so we will trust Him, and other times He hides it from us because we will get in the way. We will start trying to dictate what God ought to do in the process and cause more delays. This is something that happens a lot when we won't trust Him and wait. After we've tried our way, He has to come in and straighten out the mess we have made.

We will save ourselves a lot of heartache and pain if we just trust in our God and go after faith, treating it as an essential ingredient in all life's choices. The Bible says we are justified by faith.

> Therefore being justified by faith, we have peace with God through our Lord Jesus Christ. (Romans 5:1 KJV)

One of many definitions for *justified* is "having or shown to have a just, right, or reasonable basis." If God is saying we are justified by faith, then that means we have a right to faith. There is a reasonable basis to faith, and it all points right back to *Him*. He gave us something we would need to strengthen us on this Christian journey because the more we trust Him, the more powerful we become. The more we trust Him, the more we tap into all the resources He has provided for us. The sooner we realize we need to be in pursuit of faith, searching for ways to enhance it, then more abundantly we will live.

It has always been his desire that we live an abundant life, and I think we have already established it has nothing to do with fame or fortune. God can and always will provide—be it spiritual things or other needs—but there is an urgency that awaits us all to find our purpose and desire to be in His will for us. We must seek and find Him so that we may learn of Him and what *He* desires from each of us. This cannot be accomplished without faith. Being in pursuit of our faith has to be the determining factor. It has to be the fuel that propels us forward. There must be something in us that desires to seek out more than the measure. We must grab hold to belief and refuse to let go. In doing this, we are striving for the finish line, which ends with faith. We must yield to the pull in our spirits and just go. Our spirits will always be drawn in the direction to where He is, but it is our souls that has to be conditioned.

So I ask, to which do we yield ourselves to?

> Know ye not, that to whom ye yield yourselves servants to obey, his servants ye are to whom ye obey; whether of sin unto death, or of obedience unto righteousness? (Romans 6:16 KJV)

We can decide who will lead and, ultimately, whom we will follow. Choosing God gives us the ability to utilize all the benefits He has made available to us. I ask this question of my reader: "If we did not need faith, if faith was not an essential tool that we would need, why did He give it to us? I will answer my own question. He gave us a measure of faith because it is the substance that stems from belief. He gave us something to build upon, and as we enhance it, that brings us further into the realm of power.

In the realm of faith, all things are possible to those who believe, and He is just to manifest to us what we can trust Him for. If you have not started already, I implore you to begin to pursue your faith. Go after it with a vengeance, and don't stop until you have embraced it to the point that there is nothing that you won't trust God for. Let there be nothing that you won't believe Him for, and I can speak with a surety that there will be nothing that He will withhold from a heart that trusts and believes. To love God is to obey God, and He desires us to have all that He has decreed. He gave us something so wondrous when it comes to faith. It is something He freely gave us so that we could walk in dominion and power. We must all be in pursuit of faith because in doing so, we will find we're also in pursuit of our God.

Chapter 9
Discussion Questions and Overview

This chapter highlights the idea that faith is a gift from God, and it is essential for believers. We encourage readers to pursue faith and understand its significance. It teaches that we must continue to go after it, expounding on the measure that was given to us, treating faith as the essential ingredient to all of life's choices; and in choosing God, faith gives us the benefits of His abilities in our lives. In pursuit of our faith, we operate in a realm where all things are possible.

Here are three discussion questions based on this chapter. The chapter discussed that we often seek happiness, acceptance from others, and more in life:

1. Why do you think these pursuits often leave us unsatisfied or unfulfilled?

FAITH IS A WELLSPRING

2. How does faith offer an alternative and more fulfilling path to contentment and purpose?

The chapter suggests that the pursuit of faith doesn't mean searching for it as if it's hidden but, rather, understanding its power and benefits:

1. How would you describe the role of faith in your life currently?
2. What steps can you take to deepen your understanding and practice of faith?

The chapter emphasizes that faith is a catalyst that leads to various dimensions in our relationship with God:

1. What are some practical ways to unlock and increase your faith?
2. How can understanding the limitless potential of faith influence your daily decisions and interactions with others?

10

WISDOM OF FAITH

In this life, we search for ways to perceive and understand. We cannot stop with knowledge if we don't have an understanding. In mankind's quest to know, sometimes we don't wait on revelations to come. We decide to draw our own conclusions; therefore, we find ourselves in situations we don't desire to be in, but what comes first—wisdom or knowledge? I will answer that question because I have seen which comes first, but let's see what the Bible says about Wisdom.

> Wisdom is the principal thing; therefore get wisdom: And with all thy getting get understanding. (Proverbs 4:7 KJV)

What would it benefit us to seek out wisdom on something we don't understand? Or how could we get an understanding without first obtaining knowledge of a thing? We are instructed by God to obtain wisdom, but to get to wisdom, we must first embrace knowledge.

Notice He said wisdom is the "principal" thing, with *Merriam-Webster* defining *principal* as "most important, consequential, or influential." So would it be safe to say God is saying wisdom is the most important and influential part of anything? Because if we never make it to wisdom on anything, we will never fully grasp the concept or essence of it; but even when we get to wisdom, there must be an understanding as well.

Wisdom comes from God:

> For the Lord giveth wisdom: out of his mouth cometh knowledge and understanding. (Proverbs 2:6 KJV)

God will provide us with all the wisdom and understanding we will need on anything in this life. We must first obtain knowledge before we can make it to wisdom. Now in an earthly sense, *wisdom* in *Merriam-Webster* is defined as (1) generally accepted belief or (2) a wise attitude, belief, or course of action. So would it be safe to say wisdom, as we know it, is an accepted belief or course of action.

Could I say, in a sense, acceptance and belief on what God says can be deemed the most important and influential part of our lives? In other words, we have to be wise enough to accept what we have heard from God and act upon it. In essence, He gives us the ability to believe by granting wisdom to us. We must have wisdom in faith; therefore, we must get an understanding when it comes to faith. The knowledge of what faith holds for us gives us power and allows our faith to flourish.

As I stated earlier, I would answer the question about which comes first—wisdom or knowledge. I know the answer to this because it was shown to me by my Lord. He showed me a set of double doors, and as they opened, inside the room was a table set elegantly with china. As I entered the room, He said, "Come sit at My table."

I started to sit at the first seat I came to, and He said, "No, come sit at the head with Me."

I went to the end of the table where He was, and He beckoned to His right and told me to sit and eat. As I sat down and looked at the plate right in front of me, I could see the word *intellect*. When I started to consume what was on the plate, immediately I slid to the next plate, which I could see was filled with "Knowledge." As before, after consuming this plate, I slid to the next plate, which was filled with "Revelation." Now after consuming the contents of this plate, I began to slide past all the other plates, which seemed not to have anything in them. I slid all the way around the table and stopped right next to Him—again this time across from where I started.

As I looked down into the plate, I saw "Wisdom."

He said, "Eat, for let me explain. When you perceive anything, it must first enter your intellect, then you gain knowledge on that which you have perceived."

After knowledge, you wait on the revelation to be revealed off that knowledge. Then after revelation, you come to the wisdom of the thing you have perceived. So I saw firsthand that we will never make it to the wisdom of anything without gaining knowledge of it and allowing the Spirit of God to bring the revelation off that knowledge. God is a Spirit, and nothing about Him can ever be perceived from a carnal mindset.

My best friend Jackie said something so powerful to bear witness to this truth. We were talking about faith, and she said, "Joyce, we can never believe God with our natural minds."

How can we believe the things He say if we try to approach Him from the natural? She said an absolute mouthful. As I stated, we can never ever perceive the things of God carnally. He is a Spirit, and we must receive of Him through our spirits. With that being said, we will not always understand His methods, but that is where trust comes in.

We must never get to a place where we feel we need to understand everything God tells us to do. We have to trust Him to know what's best for us. When the time comes for Him to reveal, then He will, but we must trust the process—trust and believe when we can't see where we are going; just following wherever He may lead us. It is His desire to lead us into the depths of faith, which does not stop with the measure. He wants to teach us to embrace the very element of faith and walk with assurance and power. We must never think that faith stops; it's ever increasing and ever moving to higher levels. God is more concerned about our ability to believe Him and trust Him for who He is. We have to develop faith in what He does and what He says. That's a life of power and authority because when we operate from this aspect, we tap in to the realm of power this releases in us.

We should never think that we can have all we're supposed to have when we can't believe the things He has said. How will we reach that level of authority without accepting *all* He has said

WISDOM OF FAITH

and not just some of it? Or we want to pick and choose what we will obey and what we won't. It does not work that way—we have to accept all He has said and live our lives accordingly. He desires to teach us all things concerning Him.

The Holy Spirit is our guide He will lead us into all truths. He is a revealer, ready to expound upon any knowledge we can seek after and give us revelations on that knowledge. He will never withhold anything from His children. Anything we desire to know that leads us to Him if we search, we will find it. Having wisdom in faith is simply accepting and believing, and this will be our course of action. We can decide whether we accept the things He say, or we can reject them.

We make the decision whether we walk in the fullness of who He has called us to be. We decide if we love Him enough to accept the terms of this faith agreement. He won't make any of us expound on the measure, but we will never get to the level of faith He desires us to have if we don't. God is merciful, and He is mighty. The depths of the love He has for all of us cannot be measured. There is nothing in this earthly realm that we could ever compare it with. He chooses to embrace His creation to bask in that love in a way that shows us He loves us. Why wouldn't He want His children to partake in something that gives them power, something that releases so many resources? Having faith produces miracles and power in our lives; we just have to tap in.

> And Stephen, full of faith and power, did great wonders and miracles among the people. (Acts 6:8 KJV)

This lets me know there is nothing we can't accomplish if we have faith in God and believe what He says. We can live our lives being able to overcome things that seem to break us. We can look at our situations through faith-filled eyes and not get intimidated with how they seem. God is waiting for us to realize the importance of having faith as a prominent part in our lives. Faith must be up front and center so that we don't live in defeat. Oftentimes we're defeated because we allow how it seems or what it looks like to be the determining factor in our situations. If we find ourselves here, we must move quickly. How we perceive God can never be determined by what we see. I'll say it again—"God is a Spirit." He cannot and will not conform to our carnal mindsets, and what we can see or perceive with our physical eyes can never depict His power.

> For we walk by faith, not by sight.
> (2 Corinthians 5:7)

We have to trust in *God*. We have to believe God, notwithstanding how or what others may say.

> That your faith should not stand in the wisdom of men, but in the power of God. (1 Corinthians 2:5 KJV)

If what someone else is telling us goes against what God has said, then we must stick with God; He will never forsake us. God will gladly accompany us on this faith journey. He will always be right there to teach us *how* to increase in faith. He wants us to know all the aspects of faith, increasing in knowledge so that we will make it to the wisdom associated within faith. He wants us to have a clear understanding of faith so that we won't think faith stops at the word *faith*. There are far more deeper depths than the word itself, and it is my desire to teach it as the Holy Spirit teaches me. Faith comes by hearing and hearing by the word of God (Romans 10:17). After hearing the word of God, then we believe that which we have heard.

In essence, we build on the knowledge we receive as we allow the Spirit of God to teach us. We expand the measure that is inside of us. We relinquish the measure back to Him by fully embracing all that it is and embracing all that it entails. As we do this, then the measure we have begins to grow. The more we trust God, the more we believe God, the measure increases, and our faith level rises. The higher the level, the deeper the power—the power to move mountains and whatever other obstacles in our paths. The power is actually in the belief itself because whatever we can believe God for, He is able to perform it. He is more than able as I know. I sound like a broken record, but it is the truth. Whatever we can trust Him for, we can have it; we can receive it. I know this to be the truth in so many instances in my life.

We cannot stand firm in the power of belief if we don't believe ourselves. I could not write this book about faith if I don't have it. I trust God, but it was birthed from experiencing so many difficult things in my life. Sometimes it was things I thought would level me, but I learned perseverance. I learned to seek Him more in the midst of my trials. When we can find God inside of trying times, inside of the pain some circumstances bring, then we have found the doorway. When we can find Him in a place of acceptance and accept His will for us and not our own, then we have walked inside of trust. We have found the key to unlock all the possibilities that faith awards. To trust God is simply believing all that He has said and allowing Him to lead, and we follow. He only wants what's best for all of us, and if we trust in that, we will never fail.

Faith in God is knowing that whatever He decrees, it shall be, and all we have to do is believe it; and whatever we desire of Him inside His good and perfect will, we can have it, standing firm in our beliefs no matter what it looks like, feel like, or seem like but just believing because He said it. We must trust Him even when we don't understand *why* we're trusting. When it makes no sense to trust, we must hold our focus on Him and believe. Sometimes we have to believe Him for things that if we start to think about them, we will tell ourselves it's not possible, but I am a living witness that with God, all things are possible. If we can believe this truth, then truly this is the beginning of wisdom concerning faith. This is the beginning of a journey worth embracing. It is life altering, and it's a path that we all should be searching for because it's a path that leads to power—a power that unlocks miracles, signs, and wonders in our lives.

So I ask of you, the reader, "Will we ever get to the wisdom of faith if we don't allow Him to teach us how? Can we get to it without the knowledge of what faith really is?" I can answer that *no*, we cannot. Because if we don't take time to examine faith and understand what it means to have it, we will never make it to wisdom concerning it. We will never come to that place of power that it offers because we won't fully embrace it if we don't accept all that it wields. I encourage everyone to yield to its power, yield to the never-ending journey that faith awards, allowing the fullness of who we can be in Him to be revealed to us, knowing as His children, the gift that has been granted.

> For by grace are ye saved through faith; and that not of yourselves: it is the gift of God. (Ephesians 2:8 KJV)

This is a most precious gift, and all of us have been given a chance to partake in the majesty of it. Let us walk in the authority this has awarded us as His children, allowing the wisdom of faith to be revealed.

Chapter 10
Discussion Questions and Overview

In this chapter, we learn that God desires us to have wisdom and understanding in all things—most importantly those things that pertains to Him and what will lead us to Him. This chapter stresses the importance of understanding what faith wields for us, understanding that *faith* is more than a word. We must allow the Holy Spirit to teach us concerning faith, giving us a clear understanding of the power that comes inside of it. It teaches how we must allow our faith level to rise high above our circumstances and how we must find the doorway that leads us to trusting and believing beyond anything we could ever perceive. It doesn't have to make sense for us to believe God; we have to make a decision, no matter what, to do it.

Reflect on your own journey of faith.

1. Have there been moments when you had to trust and believe in something that seemed impossible or went against common wisdom?
2. How did your faith evolve in those situations, and what did you learn about the wisdom of faith in your experiences?
3. Do you now have a more clear understanding of what it means to have faith?
4. It is God's desire that we understand that *faith* goes beyond the actual word. How would you describe that *faith* is more than just a word?

11

WONDER OF FAITH

As we walk daily, basking in the knowledge of who God is, we live with a spirit of expectancy. We all, as His children, expect God to do all that He has promised in His Word. If we believe all that He has said, then our faith begins to find new levels in Him. God is sure, He is everlasting; and whatever He says, we can put all trust in it.

But how can I get there, Joyce, when everything is falling apart around me? How do I find a place of refuge in all this chaos breaking loose in my life?

Glad you asked. The key to getting there is *focus* and *belief*. Within any situation we find ourselves in, God has to remain in the midst of it. The main focus has to be on Him and not the situation itself, and how we do this is to get inside His Word and see *what* He says. Then we have to make the decision to *believe* what He says and act on it. The way we act on it is to trust Him and apply it accordingly. In doing this, we don't have time to accept defeat. We are more focused on trust and what He has said than we are on, what we're going through.

When we do this, we shift the focus back to God and not the circumstance. Therefore, if our focus is on God, where it should be, in any situation, we don't predetermine the outcome. As I've said, oftentimes we talk ourselves right out of breakthroughs and seeing His power with our mindsets because we focus more on what it looks like or how it seems we have already decided the outcome, therefore rendering God out of it. We must change our perceptiveness if we find ourselves here. We cannot be exuberant in our faith walk if we don't allow God to show Himself to be the God He is. If we can't place our trust in the things He says, then we will never grow to the level of faith He seeks from us all. Trusting Him is the key, and He is faithful to do all things.

> Commit thy way unto the LORD; Trust also in him;
> And he shall bring it to pass. (Psalm 37:5 KJV)

If our thought process cannot go beyond what we can see, where will we find God if we're relying on "seeing" Him move? If this be the case, we're depending on observation. We are more dependent upon what we can grab hold of naturally than what we can perceive spiritually.

As I have said previously, God is a Spirit, and we cannot approach Him with a carnal mindset. We must perceive the things of God from our spirits, which will render them powerful and limitless. If we try to approach them any other way, then we will pull them downward into the realm of unbelief, therefore talking ourselves out of what He has said and looking at things to be impossible because we start to wonder about it.

This brings us to the "wonder of faith." The aspect of wonder I'm trying to clarify here: *Merriam-Webster* defines *wonder* as "a feeling of doubt or uncertainty," and this is what we experience sometimes when it comes to faith. We have doubts; we have fears and uncertainty. We find it hard sometimes to trust God because what we are facing seems more overwhelming than what we can believe. What we can observe in the situations usually outweighs where we find ourselves, and this can easily happen when we're caught off guard suddenly, without warning by some unforeseen occurrence in our lives.

We must not give up if we find ourselves in this spot; the solution to this—"*move*."

We must make the decision right then and there to move away from fear and uncertainty. We already know God did not give us a spirit of fear. I'll say it again—fear does *not* come from God.

> For God hath not given us the spirit of fear; but of power, and of love, and of a sound mind. (2 Timothy 1:7 KJV)

Once we can get this truth in our spirits, then we can be certain when fear arises, we can quickly dispel it. Because if we can take fear out of the equation first, we are more apt to be able to focus, and we've already established that focus needs to be on the Lord in any situation. Normally doubt comes when we deem the trial too big, but can we ask ourselves, "Is anything too hard for God?" I can answer with a surety—"*no*." I promise you if we can focus on God, we will not even see the circumstance—that's just how small it will become to us.

We must never doubt God's ability to do anything on our behalf. He is able to perform every word He has spoken. Doubt will birth uncertainty, but do we really realize what it means to have doubt? I desire clarity for the reader, and I always stress sometimes we don't get the full meaning until we break words down. *Merriam-Webster* defines *doubt* as (1) to call into question the truth of, (2a) to lack confidence in, (2b) to consider unlikely. With all these definitions of *doubt*, is this what we want to tell God when we doubt what He says or His ability to perform what He says? Let me paraphrase, and I'm sure it will hit home: "Lord, I call to question everything You say because I lack confidence in it and I consider it very unlikely to happen." Can we not see the injustice of what we are actually saying when we doubt Him? Have we ever really took the time to see what it means to have doubt when it comes to Him? Is this the territory as a believer, as His children, we would want to be in? Surely not—we should never have doubts when it comes to our Lord.

One thing is for sure if we love Him—this will have a profound impact in the future with how we can believe. This will surely propel us to a place of trust because we wouldn't want to be found in such a magnitude of unbelief. We must be anchored in our trust and belief. Trusting God closes the door on doubt, therefore rendering it powerless. When we make the decision to trust Him, we realize uncertainty doesn't have a companion; and since it's spawn from doubt, then it has no entryway. We can clearly see when we don't trust our Father there are all kinds of doorways and entryways the enemy will try and use to come in. Loving our Father enough to trust Him is the game changer because when we stand firmly on the promises of God, He is bound by Himself to perform *all* that He has said.

> I have sworn by myself, the word is gone out of my mouth in righteousness, and shall not return, That unto me every knee shall bow, every tongue shall swear. (Isaiah 45:23 KJV)

He is God, and everything He says in His Word shall be; it is up to us to believe it. It truly is life altering to know Him in the fullness of who He is. To know we have a Father that is faithful to do all He has purposed is mind blowing especially when we know He has sworn by Himself that every word out of His mouth will not return to Him void. Think about what I'm saying here—*every* word He has spoken we can believe because it will accomplish what He said it will. There is power in faith and belief, and we must find a way to get there if we are to be the powerful beings He intended us to be, but as I've said, it is a decision we must all make within ourselves. I cannot have faith for you, but I can encourage you in your faith. I can teach what the Holy Spirit teaches me about faith. I can lead you to the doors concerning faith and even show you how to open them, but the decision to come inside them lies with each and every one of you.

God has given us all free will, and that involves choices we must make in this life.

Does He want us to believe Him? Yes, He does. Is trusting Him also what He desires? Yes, it is? Ultimately, we have to decide whether we travel this path or not. My faith was tested when my sister found a lump in her breast. When God told me to lay hands on her and pray, I did as He instructed. As I prayed, I reminded God of who He is and what He has said. I did not approach Him with a spirit of fear. I did not approach Him in doubt. I came to Him, acknowledging Him to be the God He is with assurance in my heart that He is able to perform what I asked of Him.

As I prayed, I could hear Him clearly as He told me all was well with her. Immediately after praying, I looked at her, and I told her, "God says all is well with you." I told her, "No matter what they say or no matter what they see, God is the ultimate judge of authority, and I'm going to need you to have faith enough to trust Him and believe it."

She declared then and there, "I do trust God, and I do believe."

She had to go the following week for a mammogram. When I was talking to God, I told Him I want to hear "benign." Lo and behold, when the technician called with the results, she said there are three spots of concern. She said, "One spot is benign, and two are cancerous."

Did my faith waver? *No*, it did not. It got stronger because He still did what I asked when I said I wanted to hear benign. I was driving home from work the day I got the news of the results, and I started talking to the Lord. I told Him, "I do not question your Sovereignty nor your ability when I ask of you. Why did this cup have to pass to her?"

Before I could get finished with the question, which He cut it off, I heard Him say, "So that I may be glorified."

I cried and cried not tears of sorrow or fear but of peace and assurance of knowing Him to be the God He is.

My faith did not waver. I did not waver in my trust in Him because He is faithful. He has proven Himself time and time again, and I wasn't going to allow fear of the word *cancer* to be bigger than our God. My sister made the decision to allow them to remove the lumps, and just as God said all is well with her, she is cancer free.

There is nothing too hard for God, and there is nothing He is not able to perform if we can believe Him for it. That was a true testament of faith being under pressure, but I was not going to allow that circumstance to determine who I know God to be. We must never approach any situation, even as serious as this one, and allow it to deter us. We must remain firm in our trust and our belief.

Sometimes He will allow things just for the purpose of what He said with her—"so that I may be glorified." All the glory belongs to Him, and it caused me to walk with a renewed strength and power of knowing what we have inside of faith. Faith is trusting God in the midst of trials, knowing He is bigger than anything we may face—which brings another aspect of the word *wonder*: (1) exciting amazement or admiration, (2) effective or efficient far beyond anything previously known or anticipated. God did exceedingly above all that we could have trusted Him for concerning my sister more than we could have anticipated. He is a faithful God, and there is nothing we cannot trust Him for. This has called me deeper into the water, and I was willing to go. Renewed strength, trust, power, and

FAITH IS A WELLSPRING

authority are my cloaks, and I will walk in all that they award me, executing all the rights He has granted to me.

God is bigger than any of life's challenges no matter what they are; we have to make the decision whether we allow them to be bigger. I have decided that what I can believe God for must outweigh any of the obstacles I may face. I encourage you, the reader, to do the same. When the enemy turns up the heat, trying to get us to doubt God, I say let's cook. Let's get out of the frying pan and get right in the fire I promise that's where He is—as we find when we read the story in Daniel when the King cast the three in the furnace.

> He answered and said, "Lo, I see four men loose, walking in the midst of the fire, and they have no hurt; and the form of the fourth is like the Son of God." (Daniel 3:25 KJV)

We have read the story in Daniel of the three that would not bow to idols and were cast into a furnace. It is a testament of the faith they had in God. In verse 17, they declared to the king that "The God we serve is able to deliver us out of this furnace and out of your hand." They trusted God, and He came to their rescue. Are we saying He's not the same God and He won't do it for us?

Can we look at all the miraculous things He has done throughout the Bible and not see His sovereignty and His power? Newsflash—"He is the same God." He is still all-powerful, all-knowing, all-wise, and Omnipotent. There is nothing too hard for Him, and if we can let that go down on the inside of us, it's life changing. He will be to us what we allow Him to be, bound by free will; but if we surrender to Him, give ourselves over to Him freely, our lives will never be the same. He is a God of mercy, waiting to reveal Himself to us, meeting us right at the point of our need for Him, always showing us that we have no need to fear, we have no need to be uncertain because everything about Him is sure. Everything about Him we can trust it, believe it, and stand on it. God never wants us to be unsure when it comes to Him. He is as solid as His Word.

We must trust and not doubt, knowing in our hearts He is able to do what we're asking of Him. We must have enough faith to wait on the manifestation, not waiting on observation. What I mean by this is when we're trusting God for anything, we cannot seek after a sign. We cannot look for ways to see if He is moving on our behalf or look at our situation to see if there's anything we can *see* with our natural eyes. No, no, no—the Bible says the wicked seeks after a sign.

> A wicked and adulterous generation seeketh after a sign; and there shall no sign be given unto it. (Matthew 16:4 KJV)

We don't need to see with our natural eyes to believe God. We can trust Him and just know. We can make that decision to have faith based off what He has revealed of Himself to us, not needing a sign, then we can act upon it and live our lives basking in the glory of who He is, never giving ourselves over to doubt or uncertainty when it comes to our Father but learning to stand firm in the knowledge of how our faith in Him will guide us straight to Him.

Chapter 11
Discussion Questions and Overview

This chapter allows us to see that our focus should always be and remain on the living God. It emphasizes and stresses that we should never doubt God in anything nor His abilities. It teaches that we will sometimes have doubts and uncertainty, but it's always how we respond to them that determines the outcome. This chapter also stresses the importance of taking God at His Word and how we should believe everything that He says because He has sworn by Himself to perform everything He has said; and lastly, even in the midst of trials, we may face He is faithful. We can trust Him for situations that seem impossible but in actuality, they are just right for Him to show forth His power and majesty.

Think about a situation in your life where doubt and uncertainty have crept in, causing you to question your faith.

1. How can you shift your focus and trust God more in such moments of doubt and uncertainty, allowing your faith to be the guiding force in your life?
2. Can you trust God enough to believe without observation?
3. Is your faith strong enough to wait on the manifestations that come when you allow trusting God to govern your life?
4. Are you prepared to make the decision to trust God instead of doubting Him?

12

FAITHFUL IN FAITH

When we hear the word *faithful*, what comes to mind? We all desire faithfulness from each other especially our spouses, loved ones, and friends. We seek that devotion and commitment that comes along with faithfulness. We know that God is faithful to all of us; there is nothing that we can't believe nor trust Him for. Now the question would be are we faithful to Him, and are we faithful in our faith walk? Do we hold to the standards He has set forth for our lives, or do we walk in disobedience and still expect for God to conform to our ways, actions, and thoughts? God will never lose His Sovereignty, and He will not share His glory with another.

> I am the LORD: that is my name: and my glory will
> I not give to another, neither my praise to graven
> images. (Isaiah 42:8 KJV)

What belongs to God is His, and we must remember and reverence that. In this life, we must let God be God. What He has promised, He is faithful to perform it.

FAITH IS A WELLSPRING

So what is faithful, Joyce, and how do we be "faithful in faith?" *Merriam-Webster* defines *faithful* as (1) steadfast in affection or allegiance, (2) firm in adherence to promises, (3) given with strong assurance, (4) true to the facts, to a standard. If we are to be faithful in faith, then that means we must be steadfast and unmovable when it comes to our faith. We must be firm paying attention to God's promises. We must have strong assurance in our beliefs and staying true to what we believe. I found myself with a decision to make staying true to my faith and staying faithful in my faith. I was faced with having to decide—would I trust what God had told me concerning myself with my health, or would I bow to thoughts given into anxiety? I had some blood work done, and all kind of thoughts were there. Will they find something? If they write me or call, then that means they found something wrong.

When I found myself in that place, I had a decision to make; and the heat was turned up when two weeks later, I received a letter from my doctor's office to call and speak with a nurse. Being honest, the old fear and anxiety returned with a vengeance, and that's when I found I had a decision to make: I could bow down to thoughts and fears, or I could tap in to what I knew for sure, and that is God is faithful. I could tap into the history I have with Him. I could rest in the assurance of who He is and what He has taught me concerning faith. It is easy for us to trust God when it comes to others or if we're not faced with actual challenges, but when it's directed at us, can we have the same faith and trust? I had to find that out for myself when my faith was tested and I was placed in the fire.

I called the doctor's office and spoke with the nurse, and she said, "I need to give you a number to call to make an appointment. The doctor has sent a referral in. Call the number, choose option one, and make the appointment."

Being honest, by now, fear and anxiety are starting to creep in. I called the number, and a woman answered the phone.

"AO Specialty and Oncology."

My heart dropped because I know what oncology means especially, as I stated in the previous chapter, what we had to go through with my sister. My mind was all over the place. I said, "Lord, can my mother take this with two daughters?"

I tried to make the appointment, and she said, "I don't see your referral. Let me send you to the one that can see all appointments."

I got a recording, so I left my name and number for a return call. I called my doctor's office back and told her what they said, and she said, "This makes no sense. I just got off the phone not twenty minutes ago, making the appointment." She said, "Let me call them, and I will call you back."

I found myself in a spot I did not want to be in because I felt myself being pulled into what was happening and focusing on what was being said to me. I started trying to focus on the things God has told me, knowing I had to find stability in *Him*, or I could easily be smothered by fear and anxiety. I began to read what He says in His Word to focus, and I began to pray.

He spoke to me and said, "You have a decision to make. Either you can trust Me and believe all that I have said, or you can stop writing about faith."

I knew exactly what He meant because in order for me to teach it, I must believe it and live it myself.

I immediately grasped what He was saying, and I told Him, "Father, I trust You, and no matter what comes, You said, 'All is well with me,' then I believe all is well."

I made my decision to trust Him on what He had said and not bow to the fear and anxiety of not knowing what I would be facing. I made the choice to trust Him, in His ability and not my own. It was the right decision because it placed me even deeper into my trust in Him.

The next day, stemming from the recording I had left, the guy called and said, "I still don't see a referral for you. Let me call your doctor's office, and if they want, they can make the appointment for you."

I still did not waver because I made the decision to trust, and I was *not* going back to that spot of anxiety.

The nurse called me back. She said, "Mrs. Graves, someone called. Were you trying to make an appointment at AO Specialty?"

I said, "You called me yesterday and told me to make one."

She said, "I don't see a referral in your chart or anything indicating you need an appointment with them."

I said, "You mean to tell me I got mixed up with somebody else?"

She said, "Apparently there was a mix-up. I'm so sorry…you don't need an appointment with them."

I was relieved, to say the least, but I had already made the decision to trust God no matter what. In the process of that, God showed me that trust is a place that we have to go and reside even when we're facing the hardest of trials. We must follow the paths that He leads, trusting all the way, focusing on Him and not the situation.

We are led to trust by the Spirit of the living God, but it is totally up to us if we come. Everything about God that He desires us to have is freely given to us.

> Every good gift and every perfect gift is from above, and cometh down from the Father of lights, with whom is no variableness, neither shadow of turning. (James 1:17 KJV)

I love the way it reads in the MSG Bible, same verse:

> Every desirable and beneficial gift comes out of heaven. The gifts are rivers of light cascading down from the Father of Light. There is nothing deceitful in God, nothing two-faced, nothing fickle. (James 1:17 MSG)

Hallelujah! But we have to receive it on our own; therefore, He does not violate the free will that was granted to us. Trust is an actual place inside of Him that we must strive to get there. There is total peace inside of trust. I have found that is where the peace that surpasses our understanding resides.

God has shown me trust is an actual place in Him because He led me there. It is inside of Him, and when we choose to put *all* our trust in Him, He leads us there. Anyone that knows me is well aware that I don't take the things God has shown me lightly. As with my previous book *My Journey into the Heavens*, I tell of all the wonderful things my Lord trusted me with. We are led to trust by the power in what we can believe. We are summoned—or could I say pulled there—by having faith in what He says. We are not forced into trust; we must come freely, as I was shown myself being pulled like an invisible magnet drawing me, but that was because I was seeking and willing to go. I was seeking because I found myself in a spot that I didn't want to be in, and I knew I had to move quickly before it could gain a foothold and lay a foundation for me in that spot. I do not presume to ever teach fear won't come or that anxiety won't come on this faith walk, but what I am here to teach it is how we respond to them *whenever* they come.

When we find ourselves there, we have to ask ourselves: What do I actually believe? Can we trust the things God has said and taught us? Can we stand firm on His promises to know that He will never leave us nor forsake us? Can we stop, drop, and roll out of the smoke the enemy has created as an illusion? Yes, we can. We can decide what we believe and whom we believe. This can be accomplished if we do not allow the enemy to pull us into the realm of sight or thoughts. We will not find faith in sight or thoughts. Faith is what gives us the ability to believe God when we can't see it or perceive in our mindsets. Faith is the manifestation of God's abilities on display, faith being our evidence while we wait for God to reveal His purposes and His plans. We are not alone; He is right here with us, leading and guiding and teaching us His ways. Once we make the decision to allow Faith to be our evidence, then we don't look with our natural eyes; we begin to *see* with our spirits.

When we begin to see with our spirits, then we do not have to see to believe we are in the realm of knowing—knowing God to be the author of our faith, knowing Him to be faithful in all that He says or does, knowing that we can do *all* things through Christ Jesus who gives us strength.

> I can do all things through Christ which strengtheneth me. (Philippians 4:13 KJV)

But it is God who has girded us with strength, covering us and securing us.

> It is God that girdeth me with strength, and maketh my way perfect. (Psalm 18:32 KJV)

Jesus is perfecting and leading us into what God has freely given. Hallelujah to the one true King. God binds us—or I could say secures us—that's what "gird with strength" means. This can only be founded in Him, but it is up to us to receive it and recognize it. We have to make a decision to stand firm in what He has given us. All that we need on this journey has already been granted; again, we have to receive it.

I understand God allowed that health scare with me to allow me to see again—this time with myself—how our faith can be under fire. The first time was with my sister, but as I said, it's easier for us to trust God when we are not the one faced with the challenges. Through it all, I had to "put my money where my mouth is," so to speak. I know with everything in me He is a God of refuge as well as strength.

> God is our refuge and strength, a very present help in trouble. (Psalm 46:1 KJV)

He is ultimately the Author and Finisher of our faith. He has given us the ability to trust in Him fully by granting us the measure of something that will, in turn, make us operate in authority and power. He showed me firsthand He is faithful in faith—faithful to perform all that we can trust Him for, more than able to perform what we can believe, faithful when we're in the fire and even when we're not. It does not matter what we face or what decisions we have to make in this life; God will remain true to who He is, and that's faithful.

Chapter 12
Discussion Questions and Overview

What can be pulled from this chapter is we all have to find a place in God that we can rest in assurance. It's about making a decision to trust God when all the facts you have goes against what you're having to trust Him for. It teaches that trust is a place inside of God's presence that we all need to find. We are actually drawn there by Him, but we have to be willing to go. The blessed part of it all is once we're there, He gives us the ability to stay.

Reflect on a time when your faith was tested, similar to the health scare mentioned in the chapter:

1. How did you respond? Did you choose to bow down to your thoughts and fear, or did you tap into what you know for sure, and that is *God is faithful?*
2. What was the outcome of your decision to trust God and remain faithful in your faith?
3. What lessons did you learn from that experience?

13

BURNING FAITH

When we think of the word *burning*, it quickly comes to mind that something is on fire or something is being consumed by fire. That is what brings this chapter into focus. Shouldn't we be consumed and burning with our faith? Should not our faith burn deep within us especially now that we have more of a clear understanding of what faith awards? *Merriam-Webster* defines *burning*: (1) being on fire, (2) intense, ardent, (3) of fundamental importance. With these definitions, I'll ask the questions again; this time I'll paraphrase with the definitions. Shouldn't we be consumed, intense, and ardent with our faith? Should not our faith be of fundamental importance? I would answer yes to both of these questions. Our faith should burn so deep within us that it does consume us. We should be completely overtaken by its power.

It is God's desire to consume us all with Himself, but this is something that has to be allowed freely by granting Him access—access to our wills, humbling ourselves under His mighty hand and under His authority and power. God is a

Spirit, and as I have stated, we must worship Him in spirit and in truth.

> God is a Spirit: and they that worship him must worship him in spirit and in truth. (John 4:24 KJV)

We must bow down in our wills and mindsets to Him, allowing the power of His Holy Spirit to teach us all things. This can only be accomplished when we submit to His will and His way. He will not conform to our idle ways and vain teachings. We must yield ourselves to the teacher, and we will be taught. He has elected to teach us about the importance of allowing faith to govern our lives.

Allowing our faith to burn within us simply means we choose to acknowledge the importance of our faith life and be consumed by it. We must allow it to overtake us and move us to deeper levels. A clear understanding of how faith can burn inside of us is the doorway to power. The Holy Spirit revealed to me that there are four other doorways attached to faith: (1) faith, (2) power, (3) trust, (4) belief, (5) forgiveness.

I asked the question: "My Lord, where does forgiveness fit in, and what does it have to do with the other four?"

He said, "You must start at the end with forgiveness and work your way back to the beginning, which is founded by faith." He said, "You must always forgive each other. To house unforgiveness in your hearts, you don't believe Me when I tell you to forgive. If you can't believe Me, you will never trust Me, and if you don't trust Me, then you will never make it to the power that's awarded in faith." Faith begets all of them—in other words, all these stem from faith, and it swallows them up.

I fully understand the concept of what He is saying. We cannot pick and choose what we can obey in His Word. He says to forgive, we must forgive.

> And be ye kind one to another, tenderhearted, forgiving one another, even as God for Christ's sake hath forgiven you. (Ephesians 4:32 KJV)

He says to believe, we must believe.

> Let not your heart be troubled: ye believe in God, believe also in me. (John 14:1 KJV)

We cannot expect to make it to the power in faith if we pick and choose what we believe. We have to accept *all* that God says and apply it to our lives. In order for our faith to burn within us, we must fully embrace it with all of God's teaching, making a clear testament to the power we will find wrapped up in every word that proceeds out of His mouth. We can see how powerful that really is with what Jesus told Satan when he tried to get Jesus to turn stones into bread.

> And when the tempter came to him, he said, "If thou be the Son of God, command that these stones be made bread." But he answered and said, "It is written, Man shall not live by bread alone, but by every word that proceedeth out of the mouth of God." (Matthew 4:3–4 KJV)

This fully allows us to see how important it is that we live by what God says. Jesus declared to the enemy that we should live by every word, and I mean *every* word that comes forth from our Father. We have learned as I spoke in another chapter that God is sworn by His own word, and it will not come back to Him void. Whatever He says, He is faithful to perform it, and we must come to a place of realization and believing it.

> Know therefore that the LORD thy God, he is God, the faithful God, which keepeth covenant and mercy with them that love him and keep his commandments to a thousand generations. (Deuteronomy 7:9 KJV)

How is that for assurance of how faithful He is? A thousand generations is past our lifespan, so that means He will remain faithful all the days of our lives on down through our children's children. Hallelujah.

Allowing our faith to burn within us, we embrace it with a zeal and eagerness, showing forth a determination to maintain it, which will be discussed in the next chapter. We must be fully aware of where we're going in faith and, most importantly, what it takes to get to the level He desires. Our Father knows we need all we can to defeat the enemy. He gave us the tools we need, which started with the measure of faith. We will always have what we need when we abide in Him and we may ask freely of our Father.

> If ye abide in me, and my words abide in you, ye shall ask what ye will, and it shall be done unto you. (John 15:7 KJV)

FAITH IS A WELLSPRING

The MSG Bible gives a clear understanding with this verse as well:

> But if you make yourselves at home with me and my words are at home in you, you can be sure that whatever you ask will be listened to and acted upon. (John 15:7 MSG)

Surely we can believe Him when He says this because there is nothing He will withhold from us stemming off the love He has for us—a love so freely given—and all He desires is for us to love Him in return and keep the commands He has given us and be committed to a life of service unto Him and each other.

> Beloved, let us love one another: for love is of God; and every one that loveth is born of God, and knoweth God. (1 John 4:7 KJV)

We must commit our ways and our lives unto the Lord, allowing Him to lead and guide us on how to be of service unto others. With faith burning on the inside, consuming us, we have the strength to accept trials and not feel the two dreadful "D's"—defeated or deflated. We will stand firm with a determination to focus on Him and not even give in to the circumstances because we can stand in power when we can trust Him. We can lean on the assurance He has given in His Word.

I can stand in power and authority and declare to you this works because I have lived it. I cannot teach something that I do not have the assurance of. God is faithful, and He has proven over and over His faithfulness in my life. That is why I can stand firm in this teaching on faith. When my faith was under fire, I chose to trust Him instead of what I was presented with. Keep in mind from the time the letter came from my doctor office and them telling me to make an appointment with a specialist in oncology, it was five days—five days for the enemy to consume me with what I was facing and trying to pull me to a place of despair, five days to think there was something going on in my body and on the fourth day seemingly confirmed as some type of cancer. In all that, I had to come to a place of trust and belief.

I prayed, and I had a decision to make as I stated. Yes, fear and anxiety arose, but I decided to overshadow them both with His Word. I began to read scriptures in the Bible to reiterate what He says. I even read chapters from my previous book *My Journey into the Heavens*. I focused on the word of God instead of my circumstance. I made the decision to trust in all that He says instead of what I was faced with. I made the decision to enlarge my territory with the power to take Him at His word and believe no matter what it seemed like. I chose faith over fear and in the end realized that was the best decision I could have made. I can say to you, the reader, "If you find yourself faced with any situation or circumstance that has caused you to feel fear and anxiety, don't fret. We have a human nature, and they will come. What's important is after they come, how will you respond when your faith is under fire?

> That the trial of your faith, being much more precious than of gold that perisheth, though it be tried with fire, might be found unto praise and

> honour and glory at the appearing of Jesus Christ.
> (1 Peter 1:7 KJV)

I can assure you if you trust God and allow your faith to burn inside you, allow it to just consume you. Let it overtake you, and make a decision to trust God's ability. Make the decision to overshadow fear and anxiety—render them powerless. The way we do this is we enlarge the territory inside of us by giving ourselves over to Him and what He says, focusing on His promises and what He declares, allowing trust to pull us like a magnet to that place inside of Him. It is a place of peace that can only be found in Him. I am a living witness that when you're faced with the biggest of storms, He has the ability to calm them. I truly believe I could not have gotten to that peace that surpasses our understanding if I had not yielded to trust Him, and it is my desire that you, the reader, knows how to get there as well. This will truly change our lives if we can trust Him enough to apply it to our daily living.

So my charge to you, the reader, is to open yourselves up to God in a way that you didn't deem possible by the power of faith and belief. Allow His Spirit to permeate your spirit and teach you how to perceive these teachings. If you can grasp the aspects of faith that has been laid out in this book, it's my desire that you be free in your mindsets when it comes to faith. The trying of our faith, the Bible says, works patience.

> Knowing this, that the trying of your faith worketh patience. (James 1:3 KJV)

Even in our trials, we will have the patience to trust God. We will have the patience to just believe God and wait. I'll always say, "Wait on the manifestation without observation"—that's my motto—because we should not have to see to believe. I choose to live by this motto, trusting in my Lord even when I don't understand, trusting when it makes no sense by man's standards but going into the supernatural realm and just believing. I charge you to allow your faith to burn within you as an unquenchable fire that cannot be extinguished by the trials of this life, a consuming fire that continues to burn when the storms of life are raging. In doing this, you will be able to rest in the peace that comes with trusting and simply waiting on the manifestation which will surely come.

Take a moment to reflect. Think of a faith-burning situation that you're experiencing right now or you've experienced. Most people would rush over to manage the fire and put it out:

- They stress themselves by finding the right doctor.
- They drown themselves in debt to pay an existing debt.
- The worst is they took it upon themselves to end the pain.

If you're tired, why don't we start now and let that faith burn?

If so, *say this out loud*!

Declaration Statement

Today, I _____, declare my intent to *let my faith burn*!

I tap upon my history with God, where His faithfulness has never wavered, reminding me that He is ultimately the Author and Finisher of faith.

I'm bowing down before the incredible power of God and letting the Holy Spirit cloak me with the cloak of faith, power, and authority.

His promises are true, and I embrace the path He's set for me, which is lit by His boundless grace. I stand firm in my commitment to this enduring faith, knowing it will guide and support me throughout life's journey.

(Name and Signature)

_____

It would be best to print the declaration statement and put it on your fridge or a place where you can easily see to remind you that you let your faith burn and is letting your faith burn!

Chapter 13
Discussion Questions & Overview

This chapter teaches the importance of allowing our faith to burn on the inside of us as a consuming fire. Allowing what we believe to be swallowed up by the power of our faith in God. It teaches when our faith is under fire gird up and trust God more. Let faith overtake us, allow it to burn within, then we can walk in Authority and Power. Giving life to what I declare to be my motto "Wait on the manifestation without observation."

14

MAINTAINING FAITH

On this journey we call life, we spend a lot of time trying to hold on to things that often seems to elude us. Then there's some that are hoarders and won't let go of anything. No matter what condition it's in, they want to hold on to it. What if we grasped this concept when it comes to maintaining our faith? What if we made the decision that we won't let go? Deciding that we will obtain all the knowledge we can about faith, accumulating all the aspects of what this life-altering journey awards us and just hold on, refusing to let go of the freedom and peace this grants us. How powerful would it be if we adapted this attribute when it comes to our faith? Through the whole process of teaching what faith is, I'm sure the question would arise: How do I stay in this place of power, Joyce? How do I maintain this level of faith without reverting back to some form of unbelief?

I will gladly answer these questions, and it's so simple until you might probably say that's too simple. All we have to do is make the decision to believe God. When we find ourselves maturing more and more in our faith walk, life's circumstances cause us to move from level to level and hold on. We stand firm, and *all* God says, we believe. No matter what is going on around us, we must not focus on it. Every time something arises in our life, we simply focus on what *God* says and let that be the determining factor in all things, allowing us to wait on His timing and not our own.

> Knowing this, that the trying of your faith worketh patience. (James 1:3 KJV)

In this we learn to accept His ways and not expect for Him to conform to ours, and we wait—wait for Him to move on our behalf, wait for Him to answer that prayer we are so diligently seeking Him for. We wait patiently on the manifestation that will surely come when a heart trusts and believes. Then we can be more concerned about what the *Word* of God says and less concerned with what others say.

When we get to a point that we can trust God and believe no matter what, then we have arrived to a place of power. This is a day-to-day process, and it's never ending because our faith will never stop moving. The more we grow in our Lord, the stronger our faith becomes. Do not get discouraged when trials come and you feel as if you're sinking or you feel somehow you have been set back. This is a tool the enemy will use against us called "illusion." If he can make us believe that we don't have the power to overcome any situation, then he has already defeated us. We wield all the authority God has granted to us inside of faith because whatever we can trust Him for—as I have stated so many times—*He is able* to perform it. We set ourselves back in our thought processes. We predetermined in our thoughts the outcome of some circumstances.

Then when we find ourselves wavering in our faith, we begin to feel like we never had it. We begin to feel like we weren't where we thought we were with our faith. This is an illusion straight from the enemy. As I have stated previously, trials will come, and sometimes they will seem hard to bear. I'm choosing my words very carefully here; they will *seem* hard, but know this with a surety—God is faithful, and He will remain faithful in all things.

> Let us hold fast the profession of our faith without wavering (for he is faithful that promised). (Hebrews 10:23 KJV, elements in parentheses mine)

He did not ever say we would not experience things in life that would cause pain, but He did say He would never leave us nor forsake us.

> Let your conversation be without covetousness; and be content with such things as ye have: for he hath said, I will never leave thee, nor forsake thee. (Hebrews 13:5 KJV)

Sometimes uncertainty will arise, but what determines our faith level is how we respond when it does.

We will face all manner of things as we go through our lives, but the things we face should not determine our faith.

MAINTAINING FAITH

It is when our faith is placed in the fire that we find the level of faith we have. We begin to see where we are by the way we respond to adversity. We begin to realize it doesn't matter what it seems like nor what it looks like; we can still trust and believe God. That is truly the beginning of maintaining our faith.

Merriam-Webster defines *maintain*: (1) to keep in an existing state, preserve from failure or decline; (2) to sustain against opposition or danger, uphold and defend, maintain a position; (3) to continue or preserve. We can see from all the definitions what it means to maintain our faith. If I were to paraphrase and put all the definitions together to bring more clarity, it would simply be this: We must keep our faith in an existing state, preserving it from failure or allowing it to decline. We must sustain against opposition, upholding, defending, and maintaining our position by continuing to trust and believe.

Simply put, *stand*—stand firm in what we are believing. Stand firm in what we are trusting. Allow nothing and no one to bring us down from this place of authority and power. God honors our faith. He honors our belief. He says in His Word what He will do when we believe.

> Therefore I say unto you, What things soever ye desire, when ye pray, believe that ye receive them, and ye shall have them. (Mark 11:24 KJV)

He is faithful to grant us all that we can ask of Him when we believe. There is no magical trick we have to perform to maintain our faith; we just simply hold on to what He has taught us. We simply believe and make the decision to keep on believing no matter what comes our way, recognizing that even when obstacles get in our path, our faith gives us the ability to maneuver through them. Our faith gives us the ability to rest in the midst of the storms, trusting with a spirit of expectancy, expecting to see a manifestation of His power, expecting to experience His glory, knowing that above all else, He is worthy of all the praise we can render unto Him.

Maintaining our faith is also deciding—deciding to hold on to what we can believe, deciding to stand boldly in the level of faith He has led us to. We must decide to stay in this place of peace, trusting when it makes no sense and even when we don't understand, trusting when everything that's presented to us goes in the opposite direction of what we're believing, trusting when everything that we're trying to hold on to seems to be crumbling at our feet. That's when we dig in and make the decision to believe no matter what. Faith is knowing—knowing God to be who He is, knowing Him to be faithful, and especially knowing we can trust Him in all things.

God has proven Himself time and time again in my life, and I'm more than confident if you, the reader, would allow Him, He will prove Himself to you as well. There is no mystery here; this is a fact. God is Sovereign; everything about Him is sure.

> Wherefore thou art great, O LORD God: for there is none like thee, neither is there any God beside thee, according to all that we have heard with our ears. (2 Samuel 7:22 KJV)

We can trust and believe every word He has spoken because it will surely come to pass in this world and throughout eternity. It is totally upon us to accept and believe all He says. Each of us tie God's hands and bound Him inside our free will, so whatever we receive concerning Him has to be willfully. He will not make us love Him, accept Him as our Lord and Savior, nor will He make us obey Him. All this has to be willfully on our parts, surrendering all to Him; and when we do this, He will withhold nothing from us. He gives us all of Himself, embracing us in a love we will never understand.

If we surrender all to Him, obeying His commands, walking in His good and perfect will for us, we have arrived at a level of faith worth preserving. When we can maintain this position, we have found the doorway to maintaining our faith. We have found the fruits of faith, what lies on the inside of it—the growth, the maturity, the reproductive quality to birth out power stemming from belief. We can boldly declare that we choose to believe Him, we choose to obey Him, and we most certainly choose to trust Him. All these things can be declared when we are maintaining our faith.

So I speak the words of empowerment to each and every person that is blessed to read this book. All that you have encountered in the pages, I decree that your spirits receive. All that God has ordained from these teachings, may you apply them to your life and live in a place of authority and power, maintaining the elevation of your faith as we patiently await the arrival of our Lord and Savior Jesus Christ.

Chapter 14
Discussion Questions and Overview

This chapter will help us understand that maintaining faith involves facing trials with an unwavering belief in God's faithfulness. The process of maintaining faith is compared to a refining fire that works patience and reveals the level of faith we possess. Maintaining faith is simply holding on the God's promises and refusing to let go, holding on to all you have learned concerning faith and making the decision to apply these teachings daily, standing firm in the power this awards while yielding to His power that works within us.

Relevance to life's experience: Life is inevitably marked by trials, and how we navigate through them determines the strength of our faith. Viewing challenges as opportunities for spiritual refinement enables us to maintain faith, knowing that even in adversity, God remains faithful. This perspective empowers us to overcome the illusion of setbacks and recognize the genuine growth in our faith through trials.

It's important to highlight the *active* decision to maintain faith by upholding, defending, and preserving it against opposition or decline. It emphasizes the need to stand firm in what is believed and to wait patiently for God's manifestation. In a fast-paced and unpredictable world, maintaining faith requires intentional decisions. Choosing to stand firm when faced with doubts, opposition, or the temptation to waver reinforces the idea that faith is not passive but requires *active* commitment.

MAINTAINING FAITH

1. How would you say from what you've learned would be the first step to maintaining your faith?
2. Can you describe what this process would entail ?
3. If you were asked the question today—"How do you maintain faith?"—what would be your response?

BENEDICTION

Behold, I come quickly: hold that fast which thou hast, that no man take thy crown. (Revelation 3:11 KJV)

I'm on my way; I'll be there soon. Keep a tight grip on what you have so no one distracts you and steals your crown. (Revelation 3:11 MSG)

ABOUT THE AUTHOR

Joyce Graves lives in Thomson, Georgia, with her husband Michael. She has four beautiful children whom she declares are her gifts from God. She loves to read and spend quality time with her family. Family is like a quilt pieced and sewn together with love and respect. She stands firm in the knowledge that God is the strength of her life, and her ministry means everything to her. To teach, strengthen, empower, and bring liberty unto all is a desire that comes straight from her heart. To allow the manifestation and power of God to flow freely through the lives of His children, she states, is truly the ultimate reward to all.

www.ingramcontent.com/pod-product-compliance
Lightning Source LLC
LaVergne TN
LVHW061550070526
838199LV00077B/6980